REALITY RELIGION
(A religion for Americans
in the 21st century)

LEO R. BOYD

Reality   House
945 Torero Plaza
Campbell, CA 95008

Reality   Religion
© 1996 by Leo R. Boyd

Library of Congress Catalog Card Number:
97-92213

ISBN   0-9660394-0-8

First   edition

Printed in the United States of America

TABLE OF CONTENTS

p. V INTRODUCTION

p. 1 CHAPTER I - RELIGION AT THE TURN

p. 11 CHAPTER II - SCIENCE AND TECHNOLOGY

p. 21 CHAPTER III - LIFE

p. 37 CHAPTER IV - HUMAN BEHAVIOR

p. 49 CHAPTER V - REALITY RELIGION

p. 83 CHAPTER VI - REALITY RELIGION AS THE
AMERICAN PUBLIC RELIGION

p. 101 CHAPTER VII - THE CONTEMPORARY CHURCH
OF REALITY RELIGION

INTRODUCTION

Religion receives increased attention around the turn of a century and especially a millennium. Religion is a subject worthy of attention. Its status in America at this time is unique in that the word "religion" has lost its content of meaning for many. This is regrettable as religion in its fundamental sense of relationships, by necessity, has always been responsible for either the success or failure of individuals and societies and will continue to be so.

The turning of this century is coincidental with a turning of my personal religion. This turning is the culmination of my personal experience which has been typical for many in this century. I was a child of the depression. I served without distinction in the ranks of our armed forces in action in Europe. I launched into marriage and family formation, shortly thereafter, with only the poor example of my home life and the inappropriate dictates of the Catholic Church for guidance. Divorce after a long and increasingly dysfunctional marriage plunged me into an extended period of personal crisis.

During this time of great stress, circumstances initiated in me a reformation of my self-to-self, self-to-other, and self-to-world relationships. I came to realize that I had abandoned my inherited Catholic belief system as a basis for my relationships and had replaced it with self knowledge and public knowledge that I have in common with most other well informed Americans. I call this new basis for the self-relationships Reality Religion.

I have composed this piece to more fully develop my thoughts on the subject of religion. Though this exercise in expression has been its own reward, I will be extremely gratified if my concept of religion provides a viable alternative to other Americans, like myself, who find that traditional religion no longer serves them well.

CHAPTER 1
RELIGION AT THE TURN

For most Americans, "religion" means the received moral code of their respective Christian sects. Though few reject the major dictates of that code or its intent, for most it seems to have become increasingly detached from the pressing realities of day-to-day living in America. Social and personal problems in our society compound on all sides. The traditional code of conduct seems an inadequate response to the problems besieging us.

Those who have abandoned the self relationships as prescribed by traditional religion have turned to a variety of alternatives. Some have adopted a crude view of our evolutionary nature as a basis of self relationships. Others have joined movements that propose that supernatural influences can be invoked which will result in a harmonious society in which peace and love will reign. The majority, perhaps, are at sea. They have no rational basis for their behavior but merely try to cope day by day.

Christian religion has failed in the twentieth century. Christian leaders of Christian countries have inflicted unspeakable horrors on humanity: mass killings of civilians in pursuit of military objectives,

genocide of unprecedented proportions, economic
exploitation of "have not" nations, and the exploitation of the "have-not classes" by the "have classes"
even here in America. Most recently, the increasing
numbers of violent crimes by young, violent criminals
who seem to be devoid of moral restraints has
caused paranoia among both the young and old alike.
It is perhaps arguably whether or not overall conditions are better of worse than previously; however,
the perception of social deterioration has destroyed
much of the credibility of conventional morality.

Many other circumstances also contribute to
the religious disaffection of the post WWII generations in America. For many of those born into the
Catholic tradition, younger than myself, the Church's
prohibition of birth control has been decisive. At no
time in history has the conflict between the moral
teachings of the Catholic Church and the pressing
realities of daily living been so stark. The Church's
stand on birth control anchored by medieval logic can
not withstand the combined assault of the realities of
monthly bills, limited living space, and human sexual
drive. Young Catholics overwhelmingly choose the
expectations of a reasonable lifestyle promised by
use of the pill rather than a life style burdened by
unrestricted child bearing or child bearing restricted

only by the impractical means sanctioned by the Church. In addition, in this time of unstable marriages, the Church's refusal to allow remarriage of divorced Catholics has alienated many more. Even those in religious vocations have rebelled against the Church's dictates on sexual behavior. Catholic nuns and priests have abandoned the Church in greater proportions than the laity primarily because of the celibacy requirement for those in religious life.

The fissure in faith created by the conflict between Church sexual dictates and common sense has caused myself and many more to examine the whole spectrum of Church teachings. We have found many of them wanting. The defections of American Catholics, both lay and religious, have become so numerous that survival of the Catholic Church in America in its present form is threatened. Among other Christian denominations, disaffection is equally great.

A common problem for all Christian denominations is that, beneath the surface of individual piety and charitable acts which is the face of Christianity, there are articles of faith in a fantastic non-material universe co-existing with every day reality. The ethereal characters of this non-material universe supposedly impact all aspects of our lives.

This other universe was conceived thousands of years ago in a time of great ignorance of physical laws and natural processes. It is difficult, today, to imagine the primitiveness of the common understanding of that age. It required a heaven and hell, angels and devils, and divine intervention to explain practically every aspect of daily experience.

For Americans, today, living in an age of technology, belief in a non-material universe that controls their daily affairs is impossible to accept.   For most, every event has a real world cause. Natural disasters are brought about by natural conditions. Disease is caused by germs and viruses.   Dysfunctional human behavior is caused by identifiable conditions either inherited or induced.   Further, adverse conditions which do develop can be remedied by appropriate human actions independent of spirit forces.

Another dynamic at work in the decline of religion is the calculated discrediting of all public morality even in small civic communities. This process is driven by people of narrow interests who clearly see that moral codes of any ilk impede their pursuit of power and money. These groups of individuals have virtually eliminated the possibility of the consensus required to sustain a public morality. They have effectively used the legal system to stymie efforts on all levels to maintain or establish community mores. Absolute interpretations of the constitutional guarantees of freedom of expression and separation of church and state in the courts have contributed to this.

The list of these special interest groups is long, but high on the list are the moguls of the entertainment industry whose power and wealth have grown to proportions unanticipated as little as twenty-five years ago. The entertainment industry has largely replaced individual and group participatory activities with the vicarious pleasures of its products. This industry knows well that pandering to the public's baser responses is a surer source of profit than quality entertainment.

People in high finance are another group eroding common morality. Their manipulation of money flow in pursuit of maximum profits can be detrimental to the general good. Both domestically and internationally, industries and regimes thrive or wither depending on the amount of financial support available from the financiers. The subject of economic justice and human welfare is rarely seriously considered in their undertakings. They hide behind an anonymous facade of a market place ethic.

Those controlling the media correctly see that

their success is inseparably bound to the entertainment and financial establishments that are prime sources for advertising revenues. Valid, pertinent information is becoming increasingly difficult for the public to obtain. Particularly, with the media becoming more and more monopolistic, information provided by the media is increasingly a commodity which is tailored to the public appetites of the moment rather than to the public's need for information.

A news topic is only as important as the media chooses to make it. Today, a given domestic or foreign situation is reported as of critical importance. A week hence it might virtually disappear from view. This is possible with a public that has been conditioned by the flickering format of TV. Perhaps the least savory aspect of the media is the outpouring of talking heads on radio and TV who depend on crudeness and over simplification to capture attention. .

The above examples of special interest groups who favor the absence of a common morality does not exhaust the list. Suppliers who cater to teenage tastes in clothes, foods, and recordings and the vendors of these items would stand to suffer financially from imposition of parental or community constraints on teenage consumption.

These self serving groups have established a

pop morality that serves their respective purposes. It is fundamentalist in nature in that it proposes extreme positions: zero regulation of their activities whether by parents, communities, or elected officials; zero responsibility for the impact of their activities, either financial or social, on society; and total tolerance of private behavior regardless of its impact on public safety, health, order, or expense. Words of consecration for this religion are: freedom of expression, deregulation, free market, and separation of church and state, which translates to elimination of public morality.

Until recently, there has been little protest of the "bottom Line" method of business even though it often works directly against the interests of average citizens. This acceptance speaks of the time and money devoted to the propagation of the faith of the marketeers and of the effectiveness and intensity of the media techniques they employ. But now, the long term economic decline of middle class incomes and increase in social anxiety due to uncertainty in the future have begun to create severe social strains. The loss of economic status in the face of record corporate profits and outrageously- high corporate officials' salaries have caused much resentment.

Ironically, those who have labored to abolish

public morality have unwittingly established their own religion, Its god is Chaos. In the absence of a common morality, many individuals, particularly teenagers and young adults, are without any organizing principles in their lives. Genital sex devoid of most human dimensions is a common image projected by entertainment media. Though the social repercussions of such behavior in society is engulfing us in a sea of problems, the causal relationship of media content to personal behavior is vehemently denied by its purveyors. The ordination of affluence and the momentary emotional rush as the goals of life has provided justification to high finance swindlers, wheelers and dealers, con artists, drug peddlers, thieves, and looters-of-opportunity.

The devotees of the god of Chaos have become a problem to the moguls of the market place who created the new god. To a significant extent, they must restrict the enjoyment of their affluence to enclaves protected by walls, guards, security systems, and barred windows. Their expensive adornments and cars are hazardous to them in many situations.

Nor are the children of the media moguls immune to the effects of their parents' pandering. The tabloids are filled with the stories of the disastrous lives of the children of the rich and famous. These children often have more difficulty finding their way than their counterparts in middle class families. Because of their parents' affluence and unstructured lives, reality for them is more remote and difficult to discern than for their middle class counterparts.

But there is reason to hope for the emergence of a new public morality from the current confusion. A large majority of people today would welcome a new morality, based on comprehensible foundations, that would enhance their personal lives and give rise to a orderly, humane society. They are disheartened by the current moral morass. They yearn for a healthy social environment for themselves, families, and friends. They are ill at ease in their solitary personal vacuums. Though they know that our earlier belief systems are fundamentally unsound, they are nostalgic for the sense of community experienced in their earlier faiths.

Those seeking a new private and public morality should be pleased -and surprised- to know that they already possess the knowledge on which such a morality can be based. In fact, the new religion will stand on just those elements of knowledge and experience which today are making traditional religious dictates unreasonable. Of course, brief reflection would suggest that this synthesis is the expected path to the next stage of religious thinking.

For the purposes of this presentation, I take my own knowledge as representative of what I call public knowledge. I am college educated in physical science though I do not consider myself an authority in any particular field of science. If there is a difference between myself and others, it is that I have had the inclination and available time in retirement to expand my thoughts on religion. The result has been this book on what I call Reality Religion.

The public knowledge of science and technology (objective reality), life (evolution), and human behavior (conditioned responses) are the foundations of Reality Religion. The public knowledge of these subjects is presented in the succeeding chapters. On the basis of this knowledge, I present the principles of Reality Religion in Chapter V. In Chapter VI, I set forth the qualifications of Reality Religion for the public religion of Americans. In Chapter VII, I discuss how Reality Religion might be properly institutionalized.

CHAPTER II
SCIENCE AND TECHNOLOGY

The explosion of public, scientific knowledge in this century has made the articles of faith of the traditional religions unacceptable to those who have given any serious consideration to the contradictions between objective reality and religious articles of faith. The non-material world of spirits and the Garden of Eden myth of creation are no longer taught as fact in the curriculum of public educational institutions, nor are they taught as fact in most religious institutions except perhaps those of fundamentalist character. The realm of public, scientific knowledge has expanded at the expense of the realm of religious faith.

Science has provided a cause and effect understanding of the vast majority of events in the our lives. Atmospheric conditions give rise to weather patterns. Germs, viruses, and other agents cause disease and physical distress. Wars and business depressions result from the actions of people. Further, it is agreed that humans not spirits control the course of human affairs.

The majority of thoughtful Americans, if asked, would agree that the forces of nature are constant and universal and that they can not be suspended by human will or divine intervention though some might harbor lingering doubts that surface during times of emotional distress. To be sure, there is still an immediate transcendence even in our daily lives; however, it is not on the plane of every day concerns and actions but in the ultimate why's and how's of sheer material existence.

The dramatic increase of scientific knowledge has contributed greatly to the technological sophistication of our surroundings. Certainly, middle class Americans enjoy healthier lives and more comfortable living conditions than their forbearers; however, it has not produced a corresponding increase in the sense of personal well being. Quite to the contrary, personal uncertainty and disquiet has increased apace with science in the latter half of this century. The hope that the advance of science and technology would be accompanied by a common perception of improvement in the human condition has not been fulfilled. In fact, as the new century and the new millennium approaches, many personal lives and entire societies seem to be disintegrating.

The lives of middle class Americans are becoming more stressful and distressed because traditional values and norms are no longer commonly shared.

Society has become more chaotic. It is often difficult to see ourselves in others. This is to say that, to date, science has diminished the credibility of traditional religious dictates, but has not provided an alternate basis for personal behavior that results in personal contentment.

The average citizen is often baffled by the failure of "experts" in their respective fields of expertise to agree on social policies. These experts have access to the same data and yet they often come to totally opposite conclusions. This has caused many to question the value of expertise in dealing with social problems. Being unable to independently analyze these complex problems, the citizen is often forced to choose between conflicting forms of political ideologies expressed in simplistic terms.

The average citizen is equally baffled by the inability or the reluctance of religious leaders to prevent or alleviate the catastrophes caused by humans which are plaguing our times. There is great reluctance on the part of religious leaders to take clear positions on human conflicts. Quite to the contrary, religious sects around the world are at the center of many conflicts. For obvious reasons, religious sects are unable to alleviate these situations of conflict.

In the last century man's inhumanity to man has increased at least in terms of magnitude. Wars have become ever more horrendous. Inequities between social strata are dramatically increasing in America. There is a general decrease in the effectiveness of educational, judicial, and political institutions. Presently, both the scientific paradigm and the religious paradigm appear to be failing. Neither provides a viable basis for human behavior in America at the turn of this century and this millennium.

To date, attempts to apply science and technology in human society have been notable failures. An early technical innovation was the assembly line. The result of the melding of man and machine was to force conformance of man to machine. The assembly line worker has been required to mimic machines. The trend continues with advances in electronic intelligence devices. Individuals are forced to interact on the terms of electronic devices. Human language is replaced with codes that the devices can identify. Electronic communication via computer is one dimensional. The subtleties and nuances of human-to-human communication are lost in the flow of literal characters on a two dimensional display. In recreation, passive observation has replaced participation - not to mention creativity. One can easily imagine a brave new world where the human character of the individual is irrelevant and only one's adaptability to electronic signals matters.

The failure of science to date has not been due to flawed public scientific knowledge but its limited scope. The public knowledge that has been incorporated into human affairs applies largely to relationships among inanimate entities or biological components -human organs for instance. Until very recently, scientific knowledge has contributed little to the appreciation of self relationships. The evolution-ary character of human beings and the influence of genetic and experiential endowment on human behav-ior has been factored into neither the self relation-ships nor the structure of public institutions such as educational, justice, and business systems.

To the degree that business leaders are aware of the qualities of human nature, they see them to be in basic conflict with the goals of efficiency and conformity. The educational leaders are largely dedicated to preparing students for the market place rather than to the development of their unique po-tential. The justice system operates on the religious concept of punishment as the proper corrective to crime -largely ignoring the social and genetic contri-butions to personal behavior.

Traditional religions' model of human nature is one based on the flawed nature of man which needs divine assistance to function and needs punishment for correction. It holds out little hope for a worldly society that -of itself- is capable of realizing the potential of either the individual or the society in total.

The discrepancy between the degrees of integration of physical science and holistic human science in public consciousness is illustrated by the easy identification of people today with behavior of characters in classical literature. The human behavior and beliefs portrayed in the world's great literary works from Shakespearian times and even classical Roman and Greek periods resonant in the present day reader. In contrast, the science and technology portrayed appears crude. A reader or viewer of these classical tales takes little exception to the roles that belief in the supernatural plays in the plots. Likewise, the characters' lack of insight into the bases of their own emotions and behavior does not detract from the drama's plausibility.

The reason for the discrepancy is that not until this century has significant scientific progress been made in the human sciences such as psychiatry, psychology, and human evolution that deals with human nature. Though there has been an explosion of information on these subjects, generally, the implications of this information to the relationships involving self or the functioning of social institutions have not been addressed.

The closest society has gotten to application of human life science to the self relationships is in the environmental movement -in this case the self-to-world or universe relationship. Environmental groups in developed countries are aware of the importance of healthy environment to the general population and consequently to all its activities. Even here, most of the efforts of environmentalists have been focused on problems remote from the masses. Urban populations and their habitat have received little attention from environmentalists. The performance of urban planners have not been any better. Stadiums and convention centers are their interests rather than plazas and promenades. A comparison of public school edifices of today with those of fifty years ago shows the current disregard for the environment of children. Many school sites built in the post WWII period look more like forced labor camps rather than nurturing environments for children.

Despite the short comings of the applications of scientific knowledge to date, the reign of rational-

ity -meaning here behavior based on scientific knowledge shared by the general public- has made great
strides in America in this century and will continue to
do so. In the case of illness, a licensed physician is
consulted. Faith in meteorology has made the
weather news the most popular feature of the daily
news. If one has behavioral problems he or she might
see a mind doctor, a psychologist or a psychiatrist,
though a stigma is still attached to this action. Particularly for people in the public eye, psychiatric
treatment is a liability -a throw back to those times in
even the recent past when the mind was not considered an integral part of the physical body and thus
subject to infirmities like all other organs. Tragic
circumstances of untimely death, incurable disabili-
ties, and personal traumas are now more likely to be
considered unpredictable events to be eased by
interpersonal emotional support and remedial means
rather than by spiritual solace.

The reign of rationality, though wide spread, is
tenuous even among middle class Americans. There
is a deep rooted psychological desire to believe in
one's ability to control circumstances by will power or
divine supplication. Another obstacle to rational
behavior is is its failure to provide the kind of emotional relief afforded by blind faith. The medical

doctor might cure but not sooth. Further, understanding the harsh realities of existence is sometimes cold comfort.

This being said, I believe Reality Religion, based on public knowledge of science, will provide the appropriate foundation for personal and social actions in twenty-first century America. This public knowledge must include the implications of the essential discoveries in the fields dealing with human life. The more comprehensive the public's knowledge of science is and the more completely it is incorporated into a society's religion, the more appropriate and productive that society will be.

CHAPTER III
LIFE

Every high school student in America is familiar with the word "evolution". The theory of evolution appears in the subjects of biology and other life sciences. The vocabulary of evolution has even been absorbed into main stream language where the concept of evolution is applied to many processes of change which occur in business and other fields. Americans by-and-large accept the evolutionary principle without detailed understanding of it in the same way they accept other broad concepts such as the "big bang" theory or bacterial infections. Only a relatively small number who are religious fundamentalists reject evolution because it contradicts the biblical story of creation and hence the infallibility of the bible.

Charles Darwin's name is associated with the theory of evolution though the idea was in the air in 1857 when his famous book, *The Origin of the Species,* was published. Its publication caused a furor which has persisted into present times. The central assertion of the book is that life forms change over generations through the elimination of the poorer adapted specimens due to competition with other life forms for means of sustenance, and by inhospitable environmental conditions. In particular, human beings, by this process, evolved from more primitive species related to today's primates -that is the family of monkeys and apes. Darwin called this process natural selection or survival of the fittest.

The most agitated among the objectors to Darwin's theory were the clergy of fundamentalist religions. The discrediting of the Garden of Eden story by an explanation of the origin of man depending on natural events rather than divine creation posed a deadly threat to the religious establishment. Lacking the acceptance by the faithful of the creation story, religious leaders would have a difficult time maintaining their credibility and authority. Fortunately for the religious establishment, the average person did not become aware of how fundamental the implications of evolutionary theory were to his religious beliefs as the choice of either special creation or evolution as the explanation of the history of life on earth does not directly impact his every day life.

The theory of evolution, nevertheless, is a mortal threat to traditional religions as it contradicts the Garden of Eden story. The garden of Eden story is the cornerstone of Judeo-Christian religions. The

God image is defined. The fallen nature of man is given as the explanation of all our individual and collective burdens. The male dominance of the female is justified. Goodness is defined as obedience to divine dictates; evil as disobedience; and the instigator of all evil is personified as the devil. The characters of the mysterious, nonmaterial universe are described, and the dilemma of a perfect god and imperfect humans is resolved by the ascribing human misbehavior to free will choice of evil -that is human choice that is unaffected by personal genetic and experiential endowment. These concepts would be difficult to establish other than by supposedly divine revelation.

The common man would have little problem with the evolutionary viewpoint if it were not for his religious indoctrination. Change is the universal experience of mankind. The oral history of any family would include stories of change from forest to field, the memories of bygone settlements, and changes in the flora and fauna in the landscape. Immutability would be a unique experience in the daily life of the individual in any age. Resistance to the idea of evolution illustrates the power of indoctrination to overwhelm even the reality of personal experience.

The most formidable scientific obstacle to

establishing the claims of evolutionists, prior to WWII, was the inability to accurately and indisputably determine the age of the fossil remains of life forms found world wide. The explosion of research in nuclear science and consequent discoveries in the post WWII period removed this obstacle.

Radioactive atoms provide an elegant means of age dating fossil remains. (Radioactive atoms are atoms with excess-energy content) Radioactive atoms emit energy and thereby "decay" into more stable states at a rate specific to the particular radioactive atom type. The decay rate of a particular type of radioactive atoms is stated as the time in which half of them decay into a more stable form - the called the "half-life." The concentration of radioactive atoms in a sample of material can be measured by proper instruments. This technology enables scientists to determine the age of both organic and inorganic materials. When the concentration of a specific type of radioactive atom in a sample at some time in the past is known, a determination of the present concentration makes possible the calculation of the elapsed time. All this is firmly established in the scientific discipline of nuclear science.

Age dating using one of the forms of carbon atoms is particularly pertinent to the discussions of religious dogma concerning man's history as carbon is present in the remains of organisms. Its particular half-life of some five thousand years makes it useful for a period exceeding the time span of both human civilization and religious mythology.

The conversion of nitrogen to radioactive carbon by cosmic rays in the upper atmosphere keeps the radioactivity of carbon dioxide in the air essentially constant. When the radioactive carbon dioxide is captured by a living organism on the surface of the earth, its radioactive carbon is no longer replenished and the concentration slowly decays away. The elapsed time between the organism's growing period and its analysis is revealed by the remaining concentration of radioactive carbon. The accuracy of this technique has been tested by the dating of organic artifacts from ancient civilizations whose ages are precisely known from written history.

Age dating of human fossils has revealed that our ancestors lived on earth long before the time of the Garden of Eden given in the Old Testament. Other age dating techniques reveal that the history of humanoid species extends over a time span of millions of years. Further, it is now established that the age of the earth and the universe must be measured in billions of years.

The Garden of Eden story as given in the Judeo-Christian scriptures is not a historical record. It is a myth. In times past, myths -highly embellished stories of historical events- were used to reinforce memories of important events. As the stories were more engaging that the events themselves, the myths often survived; but the actual history was forgotten. Perhaps the Garden of Eden story is a myth related to the period of plenty which followed the advent of intensive agriculture in the Tigris and Euphrates valleys.

A process of logical regression points to a time prior to which no life existed on earth. An era of an inanimate earth is verified by age dating the very oldest of fossils and ancient earth samples with no organic component. It is impossible to over empha- size the importance and significance of this point in time in the evolution of the universe. The occurrence of a chemical substance with a structure that had the capability and the inner necessity to perpetuate itself was an event of enormous import. This substance was the emergence of life and subsequent human consciousness on earth. The likelihood of the occur- rence of life is so small that it could well be a unique event in the universe.

The virtue of the evolutionary story of the

universe over the creationist story is not its plausibility. They are equally fantastic. The virtue of the evolutionary story is that it is substantiated by scientific evidence. There is no credible evidence to support divine-creation dogma, but there is an ever increasing body of evidence supporting evolution. The fossil collection of ancient forms of life continues to accumulate; however, as in regards to the big bang theory of the origin of the universe, the beginnings of life will probably remain beyond definitive description by science.

Evolutionary theory itself continues to evolve. As the evidence accumulates, theory modifications are proposed to bring theory and fact into closer agreement; however, questions remain. The details of the evolution of birds from reptiles, which is an important link in the evolutionary chain, is still strongly debated. The importance of natural occurrences such as ice ages, atmospheric changes caused by volcanoes, and meteor impacts on the earth relative to natural selection is unresolved. The time of occurrence of human like creatures is continually being pushed back in time. The interdependence of evolution and socialization has just recently been appreciated. Perhaps the only truly common agreement among life scientists is the necessity for the theory.

Evolution as a simply a matter of survival of
the fittest on the individual level is a gross oversim-
plification. Of course, individual survival is crucial to
the process but only as it contributes to perpetuation
of the species. Some of the most vulnerable species
on the individual level, such as the ant or cockroach,
have tremendous species-survival potential.

Consideration of social species such as humans, monkeys, and whales adds additional and
surprising dimensions to the evolutionary process.
Survival of a group or herd requires a balance of
capabilities among its members. Evolution processes
have favored much individual specialization among
the more highly developed social species.

The most ancient and perhaps the most dis-
tinctive differentiation is that of male and female.
This intra-species specialization occurred billions of
years ago when life was still confined to the bottom
of the sea. The survivability of bimodal sex forms of
some species -that is species in which the large
majority of individuals are distinctively either male or
female- evidently exceeded that of unisexual or
asexual forms -particularly for the more evolved
species.

The emergence of bimodal sexuality involved

fundamental changes in the members of the species. The physiology of the members of the affected species diverged into male and female forms. It was of necessity also accompanied by the appearance of genetic based drives which assured copulation and procreation. These sexual drives had to be very strong to assure copulation under adverse conditions. The male and female drives were also, of necessity complimentary. Only the drives necessary for personal survival exceed in intensity those which support bisexual reproduction. For some species, copulation is the last act of life. Salmon die after spawning, and butterflies die after mating and egg laying.

Sexual drives are a major factor in human behavior. They are moderated by mores established in civilized society to maintain social order. In America, the traditional sexual norms have been questioned and rejected by many. We are slowly rediscovering that norms are needed to limit the extremes of sexual behavior. Social constraints on sexuality, in the future, will need to factor in both the nature of human sexual drives which change very slowly and the social-environment which has changed radically in the last few decades.

One sobering, but undeniable axiom of evolution is: life for the individual organism is a continuous competitive struggle with the physical environment and with competing organisms both of the same and different species. Among the more evolved species, especially humans, this entails a conscious and subconscious seeking for stratagems of advantage on all levels of society -among family members, families, clans, tribes, races and species.

The evolutionary process is commonly thought of as an unidirectional one resulting in ever increasing complexity and refinement; however, evolution can result in decreased capability if environmental pressures favor regression. Neanderthal man's brain size might have been larger than modern man's. Fish that happen to have found a niche in lightless caves, over time, first lose their sight then their eyes. And the dark ages and archeological digs remind us that civilizations can decline and even cease to exist. The evolutionary process -in its self- is no assurance that the future will bring with it advanced individuals or societies or even that our species will endure indefinitely.

There are puzzling aspects of human evolution which reveal the incompleteness of the current theory. Homo sapiens' development poses problems to the basic assumption of evolution being a selection process among randomly occurring variations of individuals. Some scientists doubt that human development could have occurred in the time span allotted to it simply on the basis of random genetic change and natural selection. This dilemma might be partly explained by the unique status of humans.

Humans do not share some of the constraints of less evolved species. The human line has special characteristics which make human evolution unique. Most species other than humans occupy a niche. That is they occupy a position intermediate to other species. An example would be the several species of animals occupying the African plain. Each tends to feed on vegetation at certain height from ground level to tree top. There would be little advantage for a species to change it eating habits in a way which would put it into stronger competition with another species. This constraint does not apply to humans who have the power to eliminate competing species and for whom no superior species exists. Humans have no upper boundary. Increased or altered capability would not necessarily diminish our survivability. Perhaps this explains what appears to be the unusually large relative difference between human capability -particularly in regards to language and abstract thinking- and that of our closest relatives in the animal kingdom, primates such as apes and monkeys.

There are other serious questions concerning the geographical source of Homo sapiens, humans. Prior to our appearance, our forbearers were dispersed over the connected land masses of Asia, Africa, and Europe for longer than a million and a half years and for most of this time lived in essentially mutual isolation. In spite of this isolation, the evolutionary paths of these groups were essentially identical -particularly in regards to language capability which developed in this time period. That this most human of faculties should appear in identical form among these isolated groups questions the basic evolutionary assumption that the minute changes from generation to generation are totally random. The suggestion has been made that the options of the evolutionary process become more limited as the evolutionary process proceeds.

Though all humans are remarkably similar, there are differences among the human races. Corresponding differences in development of animal subspecies populations separated geographically and consequently exposed to different environments was key evidence for Darwin's evolutionary hypothesis which assumed spontaneous, random, minute variations from generation to generation. These minute spontaneous variations -or mutations- were his explanation for the divergence of species over long periods of time. The significance and importance of genetic differences among humans is a highly charged subject both ethically and practically. The possibility of controlling characteristics of a species by selection has long been familiar. Breeders of domestic animals such as dogs and cattle have a long history of carefully choosing breeding stock to increase the likelihood of desired characteristics in the strain.

The biological mechanism responsible for evolution and heredity was not definitively described until the 1950's. A long, fascinating scientific search lead to the definitive description of the molecular composition and structure of DNA. This chemical form, which is present in every living cell of an organism, carries the information required for the organism to grow from a single fertilized cell into the fully developed organism. The amount of information required staggers the imagination.

DNA has the structure of a molecular ladder. The rungs of this ladder, by virtue of the sequencing of their four forms, encode the information required for the organism to develop. Because this structure is on the scale of organic molecules, the directions for the development of the human being can be contained in the nucleus of a single cell. The information density encoded by DNA is truly astounding.

Further research has revealed the biological
process by which characteristics are passed from
parents to child. Both female egg cells and male
sperm cells carry the DNA of the respective parent.
In the fertilization of a mother's egg by a male's
sperm, the DNA of both parents are incorporated
into the same cell. In a very complex selection process, DNA segments carrying coding for specific
characteristics of mother or father combine to form
the complete DNA of the new individual.

The process of evolution works to develop
what I call an "organismic" species. That is a species
which is continuously moving in the direction of
perfect adaption to its environment. Of course, this
is a moving target; but, in the process, features that
are advantageous survive and features that are
detrimental or rendered useless by change in environment are eliminated. This process has the ideal of
totally integrated or organismic life forms perfectly
adapted to their environment.

In our own times, we have reached the stage
where we can significantly affect the earth's environment which means that he can influence the evolution of our own and other species. More directly, we
have developed technology to change the DNA cod-

ing in the cells of organisms by adding, deleting, or altering DNA segments -that is gene sequences. Techniques have already been officially approved for altering the character of plants and animals. Amazingly, plant characteristics can be transferred to animals and visa versa. Similar alterations of the humans genome are given a great amount of scrutiny before approval. It is not hard to imagine that such alterations are tantalizing undertakings for bio-engineers.

Technology has also created other avenues for evolutionary change. Devices have been developed that have human like capabilities. Robots that improve on the performance of humans for high precision jobs as well as repetitive and hazardous jobs are common. Literally millions of human employees have been displaced by devices with electronic intelligence. Today, it's more likely that I will be connected to a computer, when telephoning, than to another human. Whether this is a positive or negative development is arguable, and any conclusion in this regard is highly dependent on assumptions. Through constant improvement, computers already exceed humans in memory capability, operational speed, and logical ability. A bizarre scenario for the future is not hard to imagine. Artificial intelligence devices might be competing entities for mankind in the future.

The public knowledge of evolution has truly revolutionized Americans' understanding of human life and with it the basis of human morality. I present the implications of this knowledge for the self-relationships -that is say private and public religion- later in this book.

CHAPTER IV
HUMAN BEHAVIOR

However the fertilization of a woman's egg by a man's sperm occurs, whether by normal copulation or laboratory techniques, an important component of the new human's behavioral patterns -that is personality- is fixed. The fertilized egg holds the total plans for the physical development of the individual. It should be realized that "physical" means the nervous system -including the brain- as well as the skeleton, organs, and muscle. Environment and the particulars of one's developmental path will determine in what ways and to what degree the potential of the individual is expressed.

All humans are not equal even at the moment of conception. At the earliest moment of time in an individual's life, the ultimate boundaries of potential development are set though there is reason to believe that even the severely limited individual rarely -if ever- reaches that boundary. Also, at that moment of conception, genetic flaws in the parents can be transmitted to the new individual. Literally, thousands of genetic flaws have been identified. Some, like a crooked finger, are insignificant; others, like psychotic tendencies, can be crippling. It is probably

safe to say that no one is genetically perfect -what
ever "perfect" might mean.

The biological hereditary system is also subject to damage by environmental factors. DNA can
be damaged by many environmental factors. Exposure to high levels of radiation and many chemicals in
the human environment, which can be naturally occurring or man made, are well known culprits. Fortunately, serious genetic flaws present at conception
often result in spontaneous abortion which spares the
fetus a severely handicapped future.

Along with the physical appearance of the
body, heredity influences much more. Heredity is a
strong factor in behavior. The respective domains of
"nurture" and "nature" effects are not easily delineated. but we are all aware of behavioral similarities
between individuals and their parents and relatives.
Research is ongoing in this area particularly with
identical twin pairs that had been raised apart from
infancy. Similarities in behavior of such individuals
point to the hereditary influence.

Some reputable psychologists give credence to
connection of type of physique to type of personality. Popular examples of those with such linkages are
the stereotypes of the aesthetic egg head, the mus-
cular person of action, and the corpulent creature of

comfort. Obviously, too much importance can be associated with such characterizations; but most of us are acquainted with individuals who closely match these stereotypes.

The determination of the genetic makeup of the individual at the time of conception is just the first in a whole series of events that contribute to the individual's behavioral development. Every experience adds to the store of data in the brain, and every further action taken is influenced by this store of data. This process continues throughout life.

Near the end of the life cycle of the individual, physical degradation takes its toll on behavior. The human organism -like all other organisms- toward the end of life begins to lose the vigor of its earlier phases. The organs of the body, including the brain, function less well. Finally, a vital link in the organic system gives way; the organism loses its organismic integrity which is the circumstance of dying; and the human body devolves into its organic and inorganic components -not ashes to ashes but fire to ashes.

Though the newborn is not a totally blank surface on which life writes its story, life experiences pervasively leave their imprint on each of us. To a large extent, particularly, in our younger years, we are passive in this process. Despite our sense of self

autonomy, most things just happen to us. We know
that the early dog bite or other trauma can have
lasting psychological effects. Early traumas can leave
us with fears that are irrational in adulthood. Attitudes adopted in early years can be either assets or
debits in adulthood. Of late, we have come to know
the devastating effects of child abuse on people's
adult lives.

The formation or conditioning of the individual
proceeds at a tremendous rate in the early years. it
is thought by many that a person's character is
largely in place as early as five or six years of age.
Later, conditioning tends to be more on the cerebral
level rather than on the emotional level. Conditioning
comes in a host of forms.

In their childhood, both boys and girls identify
with people in their lives. Today, more than ever,
these personalities are more likely to be media images than actual people. These media images are
much more familiar to children than a local fireman,
policeman, or nurse. The usefulness of media images
is limited. They often appear in situations far removed from the reality of the child's life. Whatever
the source of the image, children unconsciously
imitate the behavior of the figures of importance in
their lives. The more inappropriate of these mimicked

behaviors might be shed later in life, but a significant influence remains throughout adulthood.

In the teenage years, idols are often peers. The cheerleader, the team captain, and those having comfortable relationships with the opposite sex are much admired and emulated. These models are generally positive ones. Less positive models models in the unstructured student bodies of large urban schools might be fellow students who exhibit un-bridled social behavior, those who intimidate their fellow students by force, or those who flaunt easy money made in street drug trade.

Much effort is made by teenagers to behave in a manner that gains them acceptance by their peer groups. In some localities, the tightest groups are the turf gangs. And sometimes gang membership appears to be the principal social involvement and protection the teenager has. The requirements for gang membership are unflinching loyalty, great bra-vado, and an adversarial attitude toward conventional society. Whether wholly realistic or not, the media leaves the public with the impression that teenage gangs are the dominant teenage social structure in many urban areas.

Traditionally, a society's behavioral wisdom has been passed from generation to generation by its institutions of family, church, school, and other power centers such as the business and political establishments Leaders of these groups have a strong interest in molding and controlling the behavior of the public for their own ends. This is a stabilizing influence in society.

Unfortunately, the behavioral wisdom of social institutions can become irrelevant to the current social situation due to its obsolescence and changes in society. Institutional leaders, being human, are reluctant to initiate change to the premises of their organizations as change usually means confusion and loss of control. When the traditional wisdom becomes obsolescent, leaders and their institutions lose credibility. When the traditional culture loses its force, a patchwork culture is created by populist figures who are unconcerned with the overall needs of a viable society and have not spent the necessary time "in the desert" to have developed new, workable bases for behavior.

In addition to behavior acquired through uncoerced choice among options such as imitation of role models or modification of behavior to gain peer acceptance, there is behavior modification which results from imposition of rewards and punishments by others -the carrot-and-the-stick situation. This type of conditioning pressure is almost a constant in our lives as something we experience in the home, in the work place, and market place. Advertising to influence the spending habits of the public is one of the largest industries in America. We are constantly bombarded by advertisements that aim to influence our choice of commercial products.

At every stage of life, others are attempting to influence us; and we are attempting to influence others. Sometimes the process is gentle and well intentioned; other times it is cruel and malicious. In nurturing situations such as a loving home or a caring educational setting, it can be benign. The proffered incentives and disincentives are gentle and the ends are appropriate. In coercive institutional settings such as prison or similar institutions of repression, it can be brutal. In the latter cases, the stick is punishment and the carrot is the absence of punishment.

Precise studies have been made, using animals -pigeons for instance- on how acquisition of behavior patterns depend on the frequency of reinforcement stimuli and how, after the incentives are eliminated, conditioned responses diminish over time. These studies have caused great controversy among eminent psychologists particularly when the results have been applied to human beings. "Behaviorism", as this approach has been called, in its pure form makes conjecture about the intention of the individual much less important in describing behavior than external inputs. Eating is seen as the result of not eating for a period of time rather than the mental awareness of hunger. Both social and anti-social behavior is seen more a result of genetic endowment and conditioning experiences than of autonomous personal decision.

The foregoing discussion of human formation seems to leave little room for individual autonomy. Beyond genetic endowment, individuals are under constant, behavior-conditioning influences. It is now recognized by most psychologists that at a given moment in time, the individual's response to his situation is largely predictable on the basis of his or her genetic and experiential endowment.

Behaviorism challenges many social and religious premises. The role of what is called "free will" is greatly diminished. It puts much greater responsibility on institutions -from home to school to church to justice system- for the behavior of people in society as these institutions control the stimuli which provide the incentives and disincentives that influence the behavior of the public. They also bear the responsibility of raising the self awareness of the public to the level at which they appreciate the importance of their conditioning on their own well being. Acceptance of behaviorism turns one's intuitive sense on its head. It profoundly affects self perception through seeing one's own behavior to be a function of genetic endowment and experience rather than spontaneous, autonomous choice.

Much, if not most, of the psychological investigations of this century has been devoted to the effects of experiential factors on behavior. The conclusions of Sigmund Freud's investigations of the influence of childhood experiences on adult behavior was revolutionary at its time of their publication in 1900. Since that time, the principle argument among psychologists has not been whether or not genetic endowment and experience affect personality but the relative importance of these factors. Over the years, the assigned scope of purely spontaneous behavior has continued to shrink. Extreme behaviorists -B.F. Skinner has been often so characterized- maintain that the concept of free will is empty of meaning.

The abandonment of the concept of absolute free will conflicts with our most personal "feelings". As our actions or lack of action arise from a mental process hidden from our consciousness, we are only aware of the external features of our situation. An exception to this is our emotional state which

can drive us to precipitous actions. On the conscious level, it seems that our behavior is only related
to the circumstances of the moment yet behavioral
studies show that our behavior is strongly dependent
on our past history.

With the increased public familiarity with psychological and psychiatric findings, the principles and
jargon of conditioned behavior has entered the public
domain. In fact, in the last two or three decades,
large, money-making, pop-psychology organizations
have sprung up that make paying audiences aware of
the potentially adverse and limiting effects of past
experience. The large numbers of paying participants
would indicate that these people believe that these
mass therapy sessions are beneficial.

When people feel that their lives are not working, they experience feelings of shame and blame
both themselves and others. Habitual mental upset
as a result of frequent, adverse outcomes in life can
be devastating. People often seek pop-psychology
cures for counter productive behavior and their
feelings of inadequacy. They often experience real
improvements in their sense of wellbeing as a result
of increased self understanding.

The debate between the advocates of free will
and behaviorism is perhaps not properly formulated.

The goal of every individual is to act is such a way as to effectively serve his or her own needs. To do this, the individual must focus on the uniqueness of his or her immediate circumstances and to act in ways best suited to produce the optimum outcome. Awareness of the influences clouding perception of immediate reality and of habits of behavior which might be inappropriate to the moment assist in attaining the goal of appropriate behavior.

The above insight can result in a great feeling of enlightenment. The insight does not reinstate the concept of free will, but it enhances one's ability to act more appropriately in current circumstance than previously. Decisions and actions are governed more by desired outcomes and appropriateness rather than past experience and genetic inclinations.

There is a tremendous investment by social institutions in the traditional free will concept. It simplifies law enforcement. People who break the law are bad and deserve to be punished. The situation need not be confused by consideration of mitigating circumstances. The broader questions of how the characteristics of society contribute to criminal behavior and how criminal behavior can be humanely dealt with can be ignored. Of course, the foundations of the traditional religions would be devastated by the abandonment of the free will concept in its pristine form. The concepts of good and evil are thereby shattered, and the thorny problem of a perfect God and a very imperfect creation is left unresolved.

Abandoning the concept of free will is also a hard thing for individuals -both the successful and the unsuccessful. The successful are reluctant to view their individual successes as a matter of circumstance rather than personal merit. They are also reluctant to face up to the social responsibilities that their fortunate circumstances entail. The unsuccessful are equally reluctant to objectively view their failures to be a result of poor habits of behavior and clouded perception. The effort to change deeply ingrained attitudes and habits is daunting even when self awareness is high.

Recognition of the importance of genetic and experiential endowment to personal behavior would result in a radically revised appraisal of self and others. Full appreciation of the import of conditioned behavior would motivate a radical overhaul of our self-relationships and social institutions. An understanding of behavior informed by reliable public knowledge is a major contributor to the exposition of Reality Religion in the next chapter.

CHAPTER V
REALITY RELIGION

The root of the word religion is the same as that of the word "ligament" -that is connection or relationship. Religion is about the relationships of self-to-self, self-to-others, and self-to-universe. In contrast, scientific relationships are between physical measurements. The humanities focus on other-to-other relationships. The arts invite us to vicariously experience the self-relationships of the artist through art forms which are often distorted by considerations of market appeal and, further, are projected through the unique prism of the artist's genetic and experiential endowment rather than the viewer's.

Reality Religion holds that, since everyone's endowments are unique, everyone's religion is unique. Traditional religions impose the self-relationships as divine dictates. The first three of the ten commandments define self-to-self and self-to-universe (God) relationships, and the last seven define self-to-other relationships.

The relationships fostered by Reality Religion are based on the recognition of the organismic character of human beings in an universe of objective reality. The merits of one's self relationships so

49

based, can be evaluated relative to their benefits to the life experience of the individual. When an individual is not experiencing a degree of gratification consistent with his material situation, that individual might suspect that his perception of reality or his conditioned behavior are adversely influencing his self relationships.

Everything that has a capacity for self relationships has a personal religion, thus we all are religious. Even animals have their unique relationships to their world. For example, some dogs are friendly toward strangers; some are not. The difference in these relationships could be the result of both breeding and training.

For all organisms, life is about developing a personal religion of effective relationships with the elements of its respective environment. For self aware humans, the scope of personal religion is an ever enlarging sphere of interaction. An infant's first relationship is to the source of its nourishment and nurturing. Gradually, the baby organizes and integrates his body into a single functioning unit. From the infant stage on, the range of self relationships, for a healthy human, continues to expand. This process is closely related to what is commonly called learning though formal education is mostly directed by others whereas meaningful religious growth is self directed.

As religion is unique to the individual, this discussion of religion is influenced my own genetic and experiential endowment. Obviously, there would be a great deal in common among the personal religions of those who accept the premise of an objective material reality as represented by reliable public knowledge. Though perceptions of objective reality vary, objective reality is a pole of attraction and convergence for those who acknowledge it to exist.

The common element in all relationships of a religious nature is, of course, one's self. The most profound impact of subscribing to verifiable public information as the basis of relationships is on self perception -that is the self-to-self relationship.

All knowledge that I now possess leads me to conclude that I am an organismic entity with much in common with all other living organisms. No factual information supports the view that I am an assemblage of body and spirit or of mind and body or of any other combination of components not organically and functionally highly integrated.

The understanding of human physiology - though certainly not exhaustive- does not reveal any organs that could possibly be transmitters or receivers of communications with a non-material world. Though the architecture of the brain has not been not been fully delineated, it fully supports the view that the brain is totally concerned with the functioning of the human organism.

Similarly, studies of psychologists and psychiatrists have not revealed any aspect of human behavior which does not have material causes, but the psychological predisposition to attribute behavior to non-material forces remains. Belief in premonitions, inspirations, and other supernatural influences is only dispelled by rational thought.

Superstition is one of the many possible manifestations of mental activity. I am not aware of any evolutionary foundation for superstition. Perhaps it is just one of the many mental manifestations made possible by the tremendous enlargement of the human brain which coincided with the development of complex human society and language capability. An analogy would be a powerful computer which was developed for complex calculations but also serves for playing all sorts of video games or for creating art work. Another explanation would be that consciousness function of our minds has difficulty dealing with its space and time boundaries. My own consciousness has difficulty accepting a beginning and end to itself and its confinement to my brain.

It is impossible to conceive of biological evolution as other than a process of development of organismic entities particularly in light of the well developed science of genetics. Reality Religion recognizes the material nature and the intra-relatedness of all aspects of each human organism.

Studies of behavior also support the organismic nature of life forms. Despite the many anecdotes of supernatural behavior of individuals, supernatural behavior has never been demonstrated under conditions of rigorous scrutiny. Genetic makeup combined with experiential conditioning are excellent predictors of an individual's behavior in a given situation.

My own genetic history is a never ending source of wonderment for me. Some billions of years ago, a microscopic yet profoundly-significant event occurred. At some location -perhaps at the bottom of the sea near a volcanic vent- life happened. A complex chemical having the characteristics of what is called life came together. This chemical array - though as elementary as it could be- exhibited the capability to preserve itself, perpetuate its kind, and express its uniqueness. From this profound and perhaps unique-in-the-universe -though at the time inconspicuous- event the magnificent panoply of life has arisen.

My personal genome is a descendant of that original spark of life. Through all the natural devastations and all the adversarial encounters of my ancestors, my gene line survived. Now, here I am: the latest generation of organic possibility.

My personal spark of life took to itself earth, air, and water from its surroundings and animated them in as marvelous a creation story as could be imagined. The resulting organism -the most magnificent type of all organisms- embarked on a developmental path of incalculable possibilities. Human life is the unbounded frontier of the universe. Only its destiny is not subject to prediction.

The career of the individual results from a complex interplay of genetic endowment, environmental influences and -most importantly- consciousness, the awareness of awareness. For the person whose developmental path has reached the point at which he or she has acquired a valid, coherent basis for self relationships and accepts responsibility for them, at this level of development, that person can cope with practically any adverse circumstance. We all know of individuals whose lives have been very gratifying in spite of extreme handicaps of health, genetic handicaps, or life circumstances. (A revealing thought is that reaching this level of enlightenment is not so much a matter of intention as a matter of having an environment which fosters personal maturation -a strong argument for a religious institution that provides the required environment).

The individual's career terminates in death which is not part of the life. Though failing of the organismic entity is experienced, death itself is not an experience of one's life but an event observed by others. The age-old concern of the living with what might be beyond the organic life cycle has often distorted and frustrated the pursuits of life. The realistic pursuits of life reside entirely within the organic life cycle.

The life cycle of each human being closely resembles those of all other organisms. Each individual life form is initiated in a reproductive process. For humans it is a remarkable process. It starts with the invasion of an egg from a female by the sperm from a male. Development of the fetus within the female's body is followed by a period of development requiring parental nurturing. After a few years, the human individual is capable of surviving on its own. Further development then proceeds in the social environment. The levels of development and expression can reach spectacular physical, artistic, and intellectual heights. An aging or degenerative process is also present throughout life and overwhelms the regenerative powers of the human body toward the end of the life cycle. Finally, a vital element of the body fails; the organismic integrity of the individual is shattered; and the body disintegrates.

I can not conceive of a more spectacular role for material in the universe than human existence. The existence of other entities pale in comparison. The roles of physical phenomena such as mountains and volcanoes or even stars are not comparable. Human existence must be the most magnificent role of material in the universe. To be an instance of life is incomprehensibly-good fortune -one that warrants the utmost respect and regard.

Reality Religion sees the highest faculty of the human species to be consciousness. It is -if not unique to humans- most highly developed in humans. The degree of its realization varies greatly from person to person. In its fuller form, it exceeds mere sensation and perception. We can be aware of not only of ourselves and the features of the universe about us but also our self relationships. We draw everything in our fields of awareness into webs of relationship which we can express and share through language and art forms.

Human consciousness integrates us with the universe. My consciousness is a field of awareness giving presence and significance to all that is encompassed. Sexuality becomes more than an response to a genetic drive. It becomes an expression of trust and generosity. Work gains the qualities of intention and appreciation of product rather than being mere necessity. And the thoughts of death and nothingness lose their dreadfulness by virtue of our knowledge that they are mutually exclusive with life.

But life is not an absolute. It is not inviolate as some fundamentalists maintain. It never has been so treated. To a lesser or greater degree, the individual's life is always subject to forces beyond that individual's control. Life is always vulnerable. Fortunately, for most Americans, the probability of an extended future is sufficiently high to warrant assumption of a future in the present. Never the less, lives are foreshortened continually in our society by a host of circumstances -accidental and contrived. Neither total acceptance nor total prohibition of abortion, birth control, capital punishment, and euthanasia are supportable rationally. The one extreme would degrade life in America, and the other extreme - if carried to its logical conclusion- would infringe on either individual or community claims. Personal choices and societal decisions are always made on the slippery slope of conflicting claims. Only fanatics and ideologues have the luxury of absolutes.

I recognize the stresses and strains of living. I am continually required to adapt to those changes which are part of my own organic process. In addition, I must contend with the many and varied pressures from being part of a social system. The problems presented to the individual by internal developmental changes, like puberty and old age, and societal challenges like economic climate and social temperament are never ending. It is reasonable to expect a life with great riches of experiences and gratifications. It is unreasonable to expect that it will be free of frustrations, trauma, and anxieties.

Reality Religion does not envision even an enlightened society to be one in which peace and love naturally emerge as the dominant features. Rather, Realty Religion recognizes that tensions resulting from conflict between legitimate but conflicting claims are inherent in nature and supports actions -both private and public- for limiting extremes of disparity and of the methods allowed for redressing these disparities.

The mere fact of my presence makes me optimistic in spite of life's difficulties. Realization that my genes have survived through an untold number of regenerations supports the view that there is a need for them in the social scheme and that they are equal to the challenges of my environment. This perspective encourages me to seek the appropriate milieu for myself rather than to struggle for self expression under incompatible conditions.

I view myself in the here and now as an organism with rights and prerogatives by virtue of being alive. The Declaration of Independence lists as divine endowments to humans: life, liberty, and the pursuit of happiness. Others have attempted to establish human rights by social contract. Reality Religion holds that the rights of living organisms are inseparable from life itself. The attributes or qualities of life constitute its rights. Living things are distinctly what strive to survive, perpetuate their kind, and express their uniqueness. Absent any one of these qualities and life does not exist. These drives operate on all levels of the organism: the biological, the emotional, and both the subconscious and conscious mental levels. The attributes of living organisms are most fully realized through their freedom of expression. Any exploitation that curtails my attributes of life as an individual or as a member of my society is an assault on my very life and justifies the use of whatever defenses are available to me.

These rights in the abstract sense are worthless. These basic rights include the rights to the biological needs of food, water, oxygen, protection from the elements, and safety of person. The ways in which these needs are met for those unable or unwilling to satisfy their own needs would depend on the economic and social mores of the society.

My prerogatives are accompanied by responsibilities. I have the responsibility to nurture my own life process and at the same time to acknowledge that others share the same prerogatives as myself. As a social creature, it serves me to actively promote social institutions that support the attributes of life.

Religion has an important role to play by influencing the character of institutions both governmental and private. Reality Religion insists that the bottom line for all governmental activity be social benefit and that all private activity -on balance- be not detrimental.

For me the challenge of enlightened living is appropriate social behavior. Ideally, my actions would be.a symphony of the reflexive, emotional and cerebral responses of my human organism. My mind attempts to integrate these several modes of expression, but in crucial situations the dominant mode of response is not always the appropriate one. Awareness of the appropriateness of my response mode is always essential for my proper behavior.

Satisfying uniquely personal needs can never be done to one's total satisfaction. In American society, our lives are currently so dominated by money concerns and by the distractions of consumerism that there is scant time for developing a sense of one's own unique needs. Further, there is little guidance in our culture for this activity. Leaders of institutions have always prescribed models of behavior that largely serve their own ends. Military leaders cite obedience, religious leaders preach blind faith, and industry leaders praise frugality to their minions.

Satisfying needs and aspirations for many -in most instances- is an unconscious process. Only when the need is urgent and its fulfillment is blocked, am I aware of the process. In American society, the din of commercial enticement can drown out the subtle, internal indications of personal needs

Satisfying my needs beyond the biological requires initiative. First and foremost, I must acquire a sufficiently elevated level of self awareness to be sensitive to those sometime subtle internal indications of unmet personal needs. An internal unbalance or unease does not carry necessarily with it an identification of the unmet need. An exploration of possibilities or alternatives to the status quo is required. Venturing into the unknown can be both exhilarating and daunting.

Resolving unmet needs often requires effective self-to-other relationships. Basic to self-to-other relationships is a realistic self appraisal. Self appraisal is generally more difficult for me than my appraisal of others. My self appraisal is clouded by own preconceptions of myself and by the expectations of others. Further, my consciousness continues to inform me that my behavior springs from the immediate circumstances. Others are more likely to see that I have patterns of behavior that are sometimes inappropriate. Ideally, I would come to a realistic appraisal of what I am, acknowledge it, and take responsibility for it.

The non-self elements of the self-to-other relationships involved also need valid appraisal. When these non-self elements are inanimate, they present less complex problems than when they are fellow humans. Inanimate objects have qualities independent of human involvement whereas interacting humans affect each other's behavior.

The certainty in self-to-other person interactions is that each participant is striving for his or her desired outcome. The desired outcome can be of infinite variety. It might be merely to survive. It might be to express an altruistic nature or just to avoid attention. Of course, it most often is to win. Genetic and experiential endowments can distort a person's perception of his or her appropriate goals They can easily make the unaware individual act out the role of victim, savior,or persecutor.

Extreme motivations are easiest to discern and assess. For instance, those who have spent a career accumulating wealth could reasonably be judged to be overly acquisitive. Similarly, career politicians might be judged to be driven by the desire for personal power and public attention. In matters of public import, it is usually valid to assign motivations of greed, power seeking, or desire for attention to the participants. Histories of wars, economic disasters, and repressive institutions support this opinion. Lust for physical gratification more often is the dominating factor in interpersonal interactions.

For individuals to have mutually beneficial self-to-other relationships, they need to acknowledge the evolutionary basis of life. The evolutionary perspective of human life presents a problem to the traditional Christian because of its adverseness and the seeming justification of self aggrandizement. The serious Christian is well aware of the pervasiveness of self centered behavior but tends to believe it is an aberration rather than a legitimate characteristic of all living organisms. That Christian might contemplate the organisms that have briefly appeared only to disappear because they lacked sufficient drive to perpetuate themselves in their environment, or he might contemplate traces of civilizations that had been extinguished because of their vulnerability.

A blanket condemnation of aggressive and acquisitive people, is not justified. They perform a very necessary functions in society. They are the ones who drive large projects in all fields of endeavor. They are able to commit their total energies to reaching their chosen goals and to extract maximum efforts from others. Their manners might be harsh; but if the goal serves the societal interests as well as their own, their behavior can be applauded. Crucial here is the balance of self benefits and societal benefits. Unfortunately, extreme self serving often does not have societal benefits.

Aggressive and acquisitive of members of society often have unbridled desires for wealth and power. Recorded history is a chronicle of ethnic holocausts, subjugations, and exploitations resulting from the actions of the greedy and the power seekers. The hard truth is that all of us are self serving to some degree and that some of us are so to a degree that is sociopathic.

In a perfect society, everyone would recognize his or her inclinations and employ them in a responsible manner. It would be refreshing to hear an aggressive person say that his natural talents were to lead and that he would responsibly do that. Commonly, leaders, particularly politicians, tell us that their motives for making the maximum effort to gain positions of power is to simply serve the masses. This motivation is contrary to the nature of those who are hard driven to dominate.

The more passive types also have responsibilities to recognize their dispositions and behave appropriately. They should identify and support good leaders and oppose those who would be overly exploitive. Each of us -regardless of our dispositions- have a role to play in society.

A football team is an metaphor for the specialization required within social groups. A football team needs a variety of talents to be successful. The line men on the team are most massive and strong. The line backers must be agile and fast a foot. The quarterback needs to be quick mentally and physically. He must make instantaneous decisions based on the situation of the moment. Then there are coaches who determine strategy and tactics and must be credible to the players. The analogy could be extended to even the spectators in the stands and those in front of TV's.

In an enlightened society, everyone would admit to consciously serving his or her own ends. Of course, in any action, one serves his or her own ends on the subconscious level even if not admitted on the conscious level. The mental function of deciding among options -though highly constrained by circumstance and distorted by experiential conditioning- is by its very nature self serving. Admittedly, the options in repressive situations can be limited to the lesser of evils.

We can not reasonably expect that we will be able to fully satisfy our needs and wants, but the individual organism -whether plant or animal- has the moral license for using whatever advantages nature has afforded it to realize the attributes of life. There is no merit ranking of means used for this purpose. Sometimes malicious cleverness has been thwarted by brute strength which though less attractive than the reverse is equally justified. A clever person is fully as capable -if not more so- of denying the rights of life as the brute. Brute strength is usually inflicted on a one-to-one basis; cleverness has often been used to victimize the many. Force of numbers has occasionally succeeded against status and power. The French and Russian revolutions are prime examples of numbers overwhelming status and power - if only for a brief interval. Economic leverage can be very effective. Gandhi sought to make India unprofitable for the English interests in India by substituting homespun for the cloth made from Indian cotton imported into England and resold to the Indians at great profit to those in the trade. Boycotts by blacks of businesses owned by whites in the American South was an effective tactic in their struggle for civil rights.

Disregard of the law of the land by the oppressed, as the last resort in a battle to protect the attributes of life, can not be ruled out. When the victimized can not redress their legitimate grievances using the rules established by the powers that be, then violating those rules becomes the court of last resort. It has played a part in every struggle between unequal forces from time immemorial.

But disregarding of the law of the land should not be resorted to lightly particularly here in the United States. We are a democracy -albeit an imperfect one- wherein legal means exist for correcting

injustices. Only instances of unwarranted, grave
infringements on the basic rights of self preservation,
perpetuation of kind, or freedom of expression would
justify ignoring the law.

Resisters of oppression who break the law in
their struggle for equal rights are called subversives,
guerrilla fighters, and terrorists by those in power.
They are thought to be activists, champions, and
martyrs by those they seek to liberate. Resistance
fighters refuse to play by the rules of the game which
they have had no hand in formulating nor have little
of the necessary skills and resources for successfully
employing.

Extremism works when the resisters are co-
vertly assisted by the victimized and the extremists
are willing to suffer the consequences of their actions. Commonly, those pushing the cause of the
disadvantaged group must be willing to risk their own
lives in the struggle. These kinds of struggles never
end.

Violent conflict between both individuals and
groups can be relieved by changes in the laws of the
land that reduce inequalities. Awareness in all quar-
ters of the substance of the conflict can be raised by
valid information supplied by the partisans. The laws
of the land must be always open to revision when

their fairness is questioned. America can be a society governed by law only so long as there is essentially consensus that the laws balance the claims of all. The burdens of extremism are readily exchanged by the members of the disadvantaged group for legal recognition of the legitimacy of their complaints.

In this century, their have been many, massive, human tragedies because those with power have for self aggrandizement denied basic human rights to disenfranchised groups under the guise of some religious, political or economic ideology. South Africa, Palestine, and Central and South America come to mind. In these areas, long, bloody wars of suppression and resistance preceded reluctant conceding of basic rights to the oppressed. A human disaster was averted during the economic depression of the thirties in the United States by the federal government's provision of the basic biological needs to the victims.

And cynicism and distrust can be excessive. We need recall that their are many complementary and synergistic relationships.in human society. Poets and troubadours have rhapsodized over man-woman affections, and the success of most social groupings and business organizations depend on cooperation and coordination of their members. Further, within the spectrum of human types, there is a broad band of those for whom cooperation with fellow humans is the preferred way of relating. These individuals are not devoid of exploitive tendencies but find cooperation is their most effective strategy.

Public recognition of the universal drive to serve one's self could drain much of the extreme emotions and actions out of human relationships. Viewing others who have claims conflicting with our own as problems or obstacles rather than as opponents or enemies allows one to employ strategies of accommodation that are more effective than confrontation and conflict though there are rare situations that admittedly can not be rationally resolved.

Mutual advantage would be the ideal goal of human interactions, but self delusion of the participants and distorted perception of reality can make it difficult to reach this goal. In slave societies, the masters often convince themselves that slavery is an advantage to the slaves. Similarly, capitalist ideologues justify impoverishment of the lower economic classes as an unfortunate consequence of the system that maximizes profits.

Reality Religion as public religion would support and promote a very civil society. An awareness and acceptance that attributes of life are inherent in the

aliveness of the individual and are not arbitrary or
bestowed by either governments or deities would be
a enlightening influence. A cultural mind set that
realizes that the disadvantaged have the moral license and responsibility to claim their rights by what
ever means that they have available would provide
incentive for all to segments of society to find humane means of mutual accommodation. It is the role
of democratic government to maximize development
of human potential by mediating the counter claims
of opposing parties and to thus preclude extremes of
exploitation and defensive responses.

In an equitable society, continuous oversight
of individuals and groups having self interests of
public import is required to moderate extremes of
behavior. The public is continually asked to believe
that individuals and groups of people with legitimate
self interests can be trusted to police their own
behavior. This appeal denies the basic characteristic
of human nature. Only careful surveillance by disinterested oversight groups can limit abuses of power
and influence by both public and private organizations
and individuals.

In contrast to dealing with overt aggrandizement, appropriate societal actions are needed to
elicit responsible behavior from the least viable mem-

bers of society. There are those whose endowments - both genetic and experiential- are such that they would be burdens on their society if left to their own inclinations. Humane incentives and disincentives for them must be provided to minimize their weight on society and to raise their level of maturity.

Working out appropriate relationships with others in the economic system is one of the most difficult and important activities of adult life in America. These relationships, ideally, would be informed by a high level of awareness of one's economic goals, an understanding of market place operation, and a thorough understanding of personal-finance management.

In modern society, our activities in the economic system are the equivalent of those our ancestors from time immemorial in their struggle for survival. The setting is radically different but the behaviors of the competing individuals, groups, and economic strata are identical. In prosperous times, competitive tensions might be muted; but, when the economy is lean all anxieties and survival stratagems come to the fore. America is now in a period of anxiety and paranoia caused by drastic change in the requirements for success in our economy. Tensions between economic strata, largely defined by ethnicity, are reaching dangerous levels.

The accommodation of the broad spectrum of individuals in the market place is essential to social stability. Unfortunately, public education and institution pretensions avoid the realities of the market place. Financial crises, both personal and broad based are reoccurring events. These crises are often caused by irresponsible behavior or disregard of the public's well being by those who affect large segments of the economic system. The majority of the population are generally unprepared for times of economic dysfunction and, consequently, suffer hardship.

Satisfying the needs for inter-personal interaction is fully as demanding and complex as satisfying economic needs. In today's highly fractionated society -in contrast to communal societies- the needs are sometimes satisfied only by elaborate efforts. The abundant, accessible relationships of the civic community, extended family, and Church no longer exist for the majority. Now, male-female contacts among young adults often are made at bars and through advertisements in the media. Obviously, there are greater hazards involved in these novel modes of interaction than in traditional modes. Young people today probably are not aware that, in the past, religious affiliation provided a large opportunity for social interaction.

Male-female relationships in the last several decades have been complicated by the lag of economic independence relative to sexual maturity. As late as the !950's, economic independence for young adults followed closely sexual maturation. Now, -for some- there can be a ten year or longer delay imposed by the need for advanced education to qualify for a job which can provide economic independence. Here again -as with economic relationships- the full support of public institutions is needed to help young adults successfully cope with the hazards, both emotional and practical, of sexual relationships.

Sexual behavior guidelines for young Americans appropriate to today's radically changed social environment are practically nonexistent. The exploitation of sex as a marketing inducement is overwhelming. So also are the hazards of sexual activity outside of monogamous marriage. Deadly, chronic, and incapacitating sexually transmitted diseases are rampant in American society. Unwanted pregnancies and the resultant children have become a major financial burden on society as well as producing large numbers of socially disadvantaged people.

An awareness by young people of the evolu-

tionary basis of species with bimodal sex -in its self-
might be a moderating influence on their behavior.
The realization that one's sexual activity is not simply
free-choice behavior but is impelled by genetic dispo-
sition might make individuals examine sexual urges in
the same light as other imposed demands on their
social behavior. An individual could simultaneously
recognize sexuality as a legitimate organic expression
and yet as something that could be acted out in such
a way as to most likely be beneficial. The individual
need not be anymore a victim of the sexual urge than
any other imposition on behavior.

It is wishful thinking to assume that young
adults have the relevant information and the maturity
to consistently behave sexually in their best interests. Reality Religion would raise the awareness of
those in the vulnerable age group of the sexual challenges facing them. It would support societal incentives and disincentives needed to reduce irresponsible
sexual behavior. It would also support accommodation of the sexual realities by public institutions via
employment opportunities for young parents and
effective and realistic sex behavior guidance.

On the personal level, Reality Religion would
invoke the ideals of mutually beneficial behavior and
personal responsibility. As in regard to other modes

of behavior, it would support holding individuals financially and socially responsible for their sexual behavior. We have been unsuccessfully in our attempt to live with the fiction that private behavior - even among consenting adults- is not a legitimate societal concern.

For many, today, the workplace provides the main opportunity for social interaction. Here are opportunities for leaders, followers, skilled workers, and many other types. Unfortunately, only a minority of people in the workplace see it as a social opportunity rather than just a hard necessity for survival; nor do many business leaders view the workplace as a context for human expression rather than an economic arrangement. Demanding working conditions and demanding managerial styles as well as employee attitudes negate much of the potential for positive social interaction in the workplace.

The satisfying of basic biological, economic, and social needs is hardly sufficient for development and expression of either individual or collective human potential. A personal religion is needed to provide the context for development of one's unique capabilities. The individual must understand the organismic nature of himself. His reality must be as free as possible from the distortions of ideology and restrictive conditioning. He must seek an environment that allows and encourages the pursuit of happiness which is to say expression. Each of us has a unique role to play. Identifying and playing this role is a worthy life long pursuit.

The individual should not rely on the social institutions to nurture his development as a unique personality though he might hope that they do not erect insurmountable barriers. A social system that purposely or inadvertently results in the vast majority of its citizens devoting most of their time and ener- gies to their economic needs -whether those needs are essential or frivolous- frustrates human develop- ment. Likewise, a society that permits the imposition of ideologies -whether religious, political or economic- on its members that block their appreciation of their own uniqueness and possibilities is also destructive of human potential. Since no society can be expected to be even near adequate in these regards, the aware individual must retain the ultimate responsibility for self development and expression.

Though the self-to-universe relationship, does not affect overt behavior as directly as self-to-self and self-to-other relationships, it is a vital aspect of maturity. For traditional believers, the universe has a material reality of some practical import and a non-material level of great importance to their situation in the present life and of singular importance in the after-life existence postulated by religious doctrine. Traditional Christians make significant investment of time and energy in the self-to-non-material universe relationship particularly in times of personal crisis. This traditional self-to-non-material universe concern diverts energies from the realities of the material situation to an imagined realm. Reality Religion adherents would be free of this concern and would more profitably devote their energies to matters in the here and now.

Abandoning belief in a non-material world exacts a price from the individual which I have experienced. The non-material world has always been a source of psychological solace to believers when in dire situations. It has offered a way of denying one's own responsibility when the demands of responsibility are too great and has been the last hope in extremes of trial. Again, human consciousness seeks survival by any possible means -sometimes by blind faith.

Empowerment that comes from dealing with reality does not always provide the solace provided by ancient beliefs nor does it necessarily guarantee desired or successful outcomes. My direct, reality based relationship with the universe, however, is

more productive than that offered by traditional
religion. I now feel one with a predictable universe
rather than being at the mercy of capricious, phan-
tom forces. Knowing that all things are governed by
the same universal forces gives me a connection to
the world and universe that traditional religion denied
me. Though the character of life is often fraught, I
now realize that I share the same inheritance with all
other living creatures and incorporate the same
materials in my body as occur in the rest of the
universe. I am an expression of the possibilities of
the material universe.

I am sometimes tempted to view my species
as the express purpose of the universe or its most
pressing concern. This chauvinistic view, most probably, is unwarranted. The human specie is a global
disaster away from extinction. Such a disaster could
be one of our own doing or an astronomical event
such as a collision of earth with a huge asteroid from
outer space. We know that there have been natural
events in the past that have wiped out great segments of life on earth. An awareness of the tenuous-
ness of life serves to make it all the more precious
for me in the midst of it.

The material universe with which I interact as a
human entity is that of human scale. It has the time

and space scale of the human organism. We evolved
to function in this realm. There are likely relevant
implications for human living in the knowledge of the
sub-atomic world and of the cosmic world also; however, to date, these implications have not impacted
public knowledge. Scientists working in macro and
micro physics speak of a sense of beauty in the
mathematical models they propose to describe these
realms. It seems reasonable to assume that reality is
consistent on all scales of a unified universe.

Humans feel an affinity with the features of
the universe. The mountains, rivers, deserts, and
numerous other landscapes excite our emotions.
With certain features of nature we intuitively relate.
Phenomena such as fire, and flowing water, that
display an infinite variety of forms are particularly
fascinating for us.

On a more practical level, we now recognize
the inter-relatedness of the condition of the earth
and our own well-being. We see, in many parts of the
world, human suffering as a result of misuse of natural resources, and archeology has revealed the remains of great civilizations that failed as a result of
environment misuse or abuse. There are many
people dedicated to a wise ecology; yet coping with
threats to American society such as excess popula-

tion, pollution of the environment, and social disinte-
gration will require a higher degree of societal commitment than has previously existed. This degree,of
cooperation might only be possible if there is common acceptance of the tenets of a public religion.

Does Reality Religion have the potential to
become that American public religion? In the next
chapter, I examine the qualifications of Reality Religion for the role of the American public religon in the
twenty-first century.

CHAPTER VI
REALITY RELIGION AS THE
AMERICAN PUBLIC RELIGION

The increase of public knowledge in this century has relentlessly discredited the mythologies of traditional public religions. The plausibility of influence of a non-material universe has been greatly reduced by physical science. Disease, natural disasters, wars, economic panics, and-most recently-human behavior are now all seen as a mosaic of interactions -well understood by technical experts and taken for granted by well-informed Americans. The present need for a viable public religion in America, however, is pressing.

It is unwarranted to speak disparaging of traditional public religions even though they no longer serve the public well. Historically, public religions reflected the public knowledge of their respective societies. The Old Testament is a prime example of religious scripture which was based on the knowledge current at its time of writing. It included health measures and social norms as well as religious duties.

Historically, religious institutions have been the repositories of all knowledge; and even when secular institutions took the lead in the pursuit and dissemi-

nation of physical science, religious institutions re-
mained the storehouse and transmitter from generation to generation of cultural mores. Even today,
religion attempts to play this role though its guidance
is to a large degree misleading because of the obsolescence of the knowledge on which its guidance is
based.

Many people falsely conclude that because
science has discredited the mythological base of
traditional religions it has destroyed the need for a
public religion. This is a false conclusion. A public
religion provides the society at large with a coherent
set of rules for behavior that facilitates orderly functioning of that society. A public religion provides a
common basis of behavior which makes civilized
society possible.

Reality Religion is a candidate for the role of
the American public religion in the twenty-first century and beyond. Currently, traditional Judeo-Christian forms of religion have little virtue beyond offer-
ing the comforting experience of ghetto community
to those who otherwise find no sense of belonging in
our market place society. The need for a public
religion serving both individuals and the society as a
whole is critical. Reality Religion has the characteristics required of a public religion, and there is evidence

of movement toward Reality Religion in our society.

A valid religion, as the basis of relationships - that is behavior-, is vital to both the individual and society. The measure of an individual's religion is the degree to which it serves that individual. The measure of a public religion is the degree to which it serves its respective society or group.

The adoption of a religion by a society depends on its ability to meet the needs of that society. In any era, there exists in any society a variety of religions competing for public acceptance. In a free society, the religion that is most suitable would be expected to become dominant in the long run. Since a "free society" is only an ideal, this selection process does not proceed smoothly.

The degree to which the country shares a common, coherent perception of reality determines the cohesiveness of that country. The validity of that common perception of reality determines the strength of that society. And that society that most-broadly shares in a common, valid reality will most likely be a humane, orderly, and potent one. It also will most fully serve its members.

Diversity in private matters such as dress, food, and art forms adds color to a society, but differences in perception of reality bearing on social mores and political actions cause stresses that can weaken and even destroy societies. Differences of opinion on slavery between people in the North and the South resulted in the Civil War -the most devastating episode in the history of America. Today, the issues of abortion, human entitlements, gender equality, and community versus individual rights are creating serious fissures in American society because we lack a common basis of morality from which to view these issues.

Rulers have always recognized the necessity of a common religion as the basis of both private and public behavior be they Christian, Mohammedan, Hindu, Communist, or Nazi. A common religion insures a unified society. The citizens of the United States of America are currently experiencing societal fracturing because they have largely abandoned traditional Christianity as the public religion and have not replaced it

Characteristics required of a religion to be acceptable as a public religion are that it reflects the people's common knowledge, that it answers the questions posed by human consciousness, that its practice promotes political stability, and that it contains convincing inducements for the many. The Judeo-Christian religions fulfilled all these requirements during their periods of flowering.

The Judeo-Christian religions are based on the cultural myth of an human like god -an anthropological god. He is a god who shares human emotions. He can become angry but can also be appeased. He demands acknowledgement, tribute, and obedience as have human potentates from time immemorial. He is mighty but has an evil adversary that is essential to his very role. We understand him. He is like us except he is perfect and his reasoning is beyond human comprehension. He is the image that the faithful turn to in the extremes of their human needs. He is also the image of authority invoked by leaders to validate their edicts.

Judeo-Christian religions satisfy psychological needs. They answer the questions inherent in human self awareness or consciousness: how did it all began and how will it end, what is the essence of human life, what happens to this essence after death, and how do we relate to the universe -or God? For all of human history, save the last couple centuries, these questions were beyond the scope of human knowledge and certainly beyond the grasp of the common man. Answers compatible with the power structure of their respective societies were supplied by those few who pondered these things. The will of God was the explanation of all events and conditions beyond the immediate actions or comprehension of the individual.

Incompatibility of political and religious institutions has rarely been a problem except in times of transition. The division of power and spoils between the clergy and the ruling class, though often under negotiation, rarely threatened their common bond which was so mutually advantageous. In most eras, the religious leaders have given divine sanction to the rulers who in turn gave official status to the Church. A very stable and mutually beneficial partnership ensued.

The appeal of the Jewish and Christian religions to their respective adherents is a fascinating subject. Both of these religions offered extremely attractive inducements to their members at the time of their formation. These inducements were perfectly suited to the conditions of the great majorities of the respective groups. Yet today, the remaining faithful cling to these inducements even though conditions in America are vastly different from those at the founding times of their respective religions .

In the case of the Semitic tribes who came to see themselves as a distinct Jewish society, the inducements were those needed by a small homogeneous group of people fighting for survival in a hostile environment of enemies both great and small: a supreme being who in return for worship and obedience would guarantee divine protection for them as individuals and as a nation against all others. For a handful of minor tribes in dire straits, this contract, or covenant, was enthusiastically embraced particularly since the fundamental laws imposed, the ten commandments, had been, in essence, already found to be workable in earlier societies.

The Old Testament is the centuries-long, partly-mythological, partly-factual history of the Jewish tribes. It is the story of many triumphs and tragedies. For the Jews to remain confident in the power of the covenant to protect them after times of disaster for the Jewish nation, they needed reassurance. This was no easy matter.

The saving feature of the Jewish belief system was that, God's favor was contingent on strict observance of a comprehensive body of laws which had developed over a long period of time. The chroniclers of the disasters of the Jewish people gave prominence to figures (prophets) who, in that time, were warning that the Jews were failing to observe the total law and would bring the wrath of God down upon them. Since strict compliance with the total body of law was difficult in all ages, a history consistent with the covenant was possible.

The faith of the Jewish believers has been tested many times in the course of their history through subjugations by neighboring nations and by innumerable pogroms in Diaspora. The loyalty of the Jews to their faith speaks to their fondness of Jewish culture and their attachment to their tradition. Only the holocaust during the Nazi regime in Germany shook the conviction of a significant fraction of the Jews. How could the Jews deserve suffering of this magnitude?

The founders of modern Israel, while not forsaking their religious heritage, recognized that deliverance depended on the universally accepted strategies of force of arms and strong allies. Dependence on divine favor was not allowed to preclude practical measures. Though this new orientation has caused some dissension among the Jews, there is virtually no public criticism of Israel by Jews for maintaining the strongest possible military arsenal in the Middle East and the strongest political and military allies possible as a means of survival.

The fathers of Christianity -though rooted in the soil of Judaism- had, at the time of Jesus, an environment radically different from the Jewish tribes at the time of the founding of the Jewish nation and religion. Christianity was founded in the midst of the Roman Empire. The Roman Empire was a huge multi-racial, authoritarian society. There was great disparity between the upper and lower classes. The lot of the commoner was harsh with little hope for improvement.

A religion that offered solace for the downtrodden would find fertile ground. Christianity was that religion. Rewards for the just and punishments for the unjust would be dispensed in a heavenly realm which was commonly thought to be located somewhere above man's flat-earth habitat. The promised, heavenly rewards were so extravagant that the deprivations of one's earthly life could be seen to be insignificant. Further, membership in this new religion was open to all regardless of nationality. The characteristics of Christianity fit well with the multi-ethnic character of and deprivation of the lower classes in the Roman Empire.

The attractiveness of this new religion to the downtrodden masses of the Roman Empire who had scant hope of escape from a life of abject poverty and repression is obvious. The grim realities of earthly life became less important then the glories of the hereafter for those who patiently endured their hardships. The pacifying affect of Christianity on the masses was fully appreciated by those Romans in positions of power

Reality checks by the Christian faithful are even more difficult to make than for they are for Jews. They are essentially impossible. The terms of the new covenant, reward for the obedient and punishment for the transgressors, are to be carried out in another realm. Only in this century, and then only in advanced countries, have large numbers of Christians decided that their human condition in the earthly realm is more important than the future condition of a dubious spirit entity, the so-called soul, in a remote realm of questionable existence.

Any religion that would emerge in the present time as an American public religion would have the same requirements for acceptance as did traditional religions at the time of their emergence. It must be compatible with the public knowledge of those seeking a meaningful way of life, it must respond to the age-old questions posed by human consciousness, it must be compatible with the social and political ideals of American society, and it must offer inducements for potential adherents. Reality Religion meets these requirements for well-informed Americans in this time.

The self relationships of Reality Religion incorporate the public knowledge of well informed Americans. Reality Religion addresses the questions posed by human consciousness. It also is an attractive option for those Americans seeking a rational and humane society. The reactions of American institutional leaders to the emergence of Reality Religion and the strength of these reactions, however, are more difficult to foresee.

Not only the knowledge of the scientific revolution but the equally-important knowledge produced by the life sciences in this century is incorporated into Reality Religion. The knowledge of the scientific revolution firmly establishes the material basis of all the phenomena of our daily lives. It informs us that we are expressions of the universe and as such are integral with it. The knowledge from the life sciences bearing on evolution allows us to appreciate the organismic nature of human life. It explains the inherent tensions which exist among all organisms even those of the same specie. Self-to-other relationships now are seen as naturally fraught with difficulties, but these difficulties once recognized as inherent in nature can be rationally and humanely managed by an accommodating legal system. Appreciation of the role of genetic and experiential endowments in human behavior does much to inform both self-to-self and self-to-other relationships.

Reality Religion meets psychological needs - that is the needs of human consciousness- with its organismic model of human life. We as humans experience a life cycle similar to all other organisms. We have been regenerated time and time again throughout the history of our specie. We the living are privileged to play the most magnificent role in the universe. In humans, the universe displays an awareness of self. Human existence derives its character and significance from the attributes of life. Its meaning is inherent in the qualities of life itself. Its claims need no longer be thought to be endowed by a non-material deity nor mere tenets of some political ideology.

The appeal of Reality Religion to well-informed Americans is obvious. It allows the chaos in our society to be seen as the consequence of the lack of a public religion that provides a comprehensible, workable basis of behavior. To Americans who seek to build on the best in our society, Reality Religion offers paradigm that does not promise a utopia buts maximizes societal cohesiveness by moderating the extremes of disparity and social tensions by demo-cratic means.

It would be expected that Reality Religion, which has the potential to fundamentally change people's perception of themselves and the world around them, is one that will be carefully scrutinized by the powers that be. Leaders of every established institution will be sensitive to the impact of a novel individual and public consciousness and will be quick to react to any threat to their own self interests. Several of these perceived threats are discussed below.

It is not hard to imagine the response of those with vested interests in traditional religions to a source of a new consciousness that discredits the very foundations of their establishments and hence their status and credibility. If ignoring and even denying exposure of their followers to Reality Religion does not stifle it, then personal attacks on individuals in the new religion could be expected. Religions -both traditional and new age- are one of the largest concentrations of power and wealth in the Country. Power and wealth are never relinquished without a struggle.

Those in the criminal justice system, citizens-at-large, judges, lawyers, police personnel, prison employees, cops on the beat- would also need to radically change their thinking. They would no longer operate on the traditional basis of punishment of free-choice criminal actions. Instead, the limited autonomy of the criminal due to both genetic endowment and experiential endowment would be recognized. Justice would be dispensed to protect the community and to humanely limit the possibility of further criminal acts by the transgressor rather than to punish. Further, habitual criminals would be appropriately restricted and monitored even after completion of sentences. Government officials would need to recognize their responsibility to create a social environment and provide for all the necessary incentives and disincentives that encourage appropriate behavior. This change in operating methods would not be welcomed by many in the criminal justice system.

Those in government would need to abandon the one-size-fits-all method of governing. Their task would be to recognize the legitimate but conflicting claims of both individuals and self interest groups and moderate disparities thus limiting the need for extremes of behavior to achieve an accepted balance.

I anticipate that the acceptance of Reality Religion by Americans would greatly reduce anger in our society by virtue of enhancing the common understanding of the bases of conflicts. They would accept that government's role is to manage conflicts as they evolve rather than solving them. They would not expect a problem free society

Traditional religions -world wide- have attempted to foster social stability by preaching docility and submission to authority even in the face of exploitation and repression. Responsibility for social justice and equity was granted to the rich and powerful. Inevitably, -human nature being what it is- justice and equity has been gained by the victimized only through their own strenuous efforts.

Reality Religion teaches that the rights of life are inherent in the individual and that the individual and his society have the moral license to secure them by what ever means available. Public acceptance of this reality produces a continually shifting but stable social balance and precludes the necessity for violence. The victim-savior-persecutor paradigm is abolished.

I envision Reality Religion described herein as a populist religion. Participants will bond not on the basis of acceptance of a received creed but on recognized usefulness of behavior based on objective reality -by which all behavior must be ultimately measured.

There would be little conflict between Reality

Religion and the American political system as both are reality based. The Constitution is notably free of ideological and mythological bases; however, in the last-few decades there has been a notable resurgence of fundamentalism in America as well as world wide. The inability of fractured societies to effectively deal with societal problems has fostered this regression. This inability is closely linked to the lack of a viable public religion.

Traditional religions are ineffectual in America. The problems plaguing American did not exist at the time of their formation; and as their doctrines purport to be immutable, their dictates can hardly be expected to be antidotes to today's personal and social problems. Today's social and economic environment as well as the technological environment differs radically from what it was in the time of Jesus or the Jewish patriarchs.

The American public would welcome guidance from a religious institution whose basis of conduct is relevant to current problems. It is presumptuous to believe each individual American would or could develop a workable code of conduct for himself on his own. There have been only a handful of individuals in the history of the world who have productively addressed the subject of human existence.

A final aspect of this discourse remains: the institutionalization of Reality Religion. An organization or an association is needed in which behavior informed by public knowledge is practiced and encouraged. The characteristics of such an institution will be discussed in the next and last chapter of this discourse. I call this institution the Contemporary Church of Reality Religion.

CHAPTER VII
CONTEMPORARY CHURCH
OF REALITY RELIGION

Institutionalized Reality Religion, which I call the Contemporary Church of Reality Religion, will have much of the form and function of traditional religious organizations. It will be an association of groups of people pursuing a particular model for personal behavior-that is the relationships of self to self, self to others, and self to universe. The difference between Contemporary Church and traditional religious sects - which is fundamental- is that the basis of behavior supported by the Contemporary Church is reliable, public knowledge rather than dogmatic, mythologically-based dictates of a hierarchy.

As the form and function of religious institutions have much in common, it makes sense, for me, to discuss Contemporary Church relative to the Catholic Church with which I am familiar. I will use The Catholic Church as a reference for form and function in exposition of the particular characteristics I assign to the Contemporary Church.

When the Catholic Church is mentioned it usually evokes the image of a gigantic monolithic structure in which all activities of its members are tightly controlled by top management. This is not an accurate portrayal. Top management -that is the hierarchy- in the Catholic Church is single minded in its intention to maintain control of that thinking and behavior of its members that preserves its power as a cultural and financial entity. Matters that do not adversely impact the hierarchy's interests are of little consequence to them; therefore, there exists a great deal of diversity among parish communities. The character of a particular parish is allowed to adapt to the particular needs of its lay members. It would be difficult to accept on the basis of appearances that a Catholic parish in rural Latin American and one in American suburbia belong to the same religious organization.

Catholic parishes can be viewed as communities whose particular characteristics have developed, relatively free of clerical influence, to meet the needs of its members. In a thriving urban parish, there are activities for men, women, and children separately and collectively. There is assistance for the needy by direct assistance and networking of resources for assistance. There are support groups for those in distress due to divorce, personal loss, or addiction.

But first and foremost parishes are human communities. The mass liturgy, which is its primary expression of Catholicism, is fundamentally a celebration of community -common participation in a meal. Unfortunately, the communitarian character of the mass was changed to a mass worship ritual when Christianity became the official religion of the Roman Empire. Only recently, has its original character been partially restored -primarily in America. The bread and wine sharing ceremony has Jewish roots, but it is also a universal ritual of community. The attraction of traditional churches has been the community experience they provide to their members. This need for community is so valuable for the members that they tolerate the impositions of their hierarchy to reap this benefit. The bonds of community have been so strong that members of Christian sects that differ in name only have waged bloody wars against each other to protect their communities from perceived threats.

The harshest punishment possible for the majority of humans is rejection by their community be it family members, club, or church. Community is the responsive reality of life for its members. Without community interaction one easily losses a sense of self. In isolation, most people become disoriented.

What should be the characteristics of the Contemporary Church of Reality Religion fashioned to

serve Americans today? Contemporary Church -in
contrast to traditional churches- would embody the
democratic forms and processes of American government. The dogmatic, authoritarian, patriarchal, and
hierarchical aspects of the Roman Church are incompatible with the pragmatic, democratic, and egalitar-
ian principles that are so precious in Western democ-
racies and that have been institutionalized -to some
degree- only at great price.

The Roman Church mimicked Roman political
forms current at the time Christianity became legally
acceptable by the Roman Empire. Those forms have
persisted for fifteen-hundred years. Even clerical
vestments are reflections of the garb of the Roman
upper class of that period. Many of the characteristics of the Roman Empire society are abhorrent to us
as Americans: slavery, mass ignorance, patriarchal
tyranny, and the manipulation of the masses by the
rulers with "bread-and-circuses."

Both the founders of and adherents to the
Contemporary Church of Reality Religion would need
to exert great caution to minimize distortion and
perversion of the intent of Reality Religion in the
process of institutionalization -the fate of the Jesus
message. It is well known that the character of
Christianity changed drastically in the transition from

a populist religion of the downtrodden to the official religion of Rome.

The Jesus message and current Church practices are strongly at odds. It is hard to imagine that Jesus would have been as violently intolerant of opposing religious viewpoints as the Roman Catholic hierarchy. Also, it is unlikely that he would have approved of the rigidity of Church dictates. Jesus' genius was his ability to address the uniqueness of each problem situation -for instance the judging of the woman caught in the act of adultery.

Contemporary Church would not try to establish behavioral norms through the exercise of authority but by raising the awareness of its members to the nuances of the self relationships. It would foster self-relationships in the light of reliable public knowledge rather than divine dictates. Norms detrimental to realization of human potential would be avoided. It would provide the forum for illuminating the problems of the self relationships facing Americans in these stressful times.

What are the problems of thoughtful Americans at the end of the "American century"? Many Americans feel that control of their lives and control of their society has slipped from their grasp. Phobia and paranoia is rampant. The efforts required to maintain life styles measured by consumption of products more and more precludes the pursuit of personal expression. Life for many of the younger generations, in this age of electronic media, has become an impersonal, vicarious experience. Virtual reality - of which the internet is a form- is the latest distraction being peddled to the public. The art of living intimately -that is living in close relationship with one's immediate social and natural environment- is being lost by many to their own detriment.

Thoughtful Americans are aware of a need for an opportunity in which to be uniquely human. Contemporary Church would that place to be among and with people as unique individuals. Many forces in American society act to eliminate one's uniqueness and even one's humanness, Traditional churches are guilty of this as well. Christian churches present a, specific, unrealistic model of behavior which all are expected to emulate. Deviation from this ideal is labeled a personal failing -even a vice. The inability of conscientious people to measure up to an abstract ideal destroys much of their self esteem. Inability to conform to this ideal often results in the believer having no model of behavior at all.

The work place suffers from similar limitations People are required to be cogs in the organizational

wheel They are valued by their function rather than
by who and what they are. The modern counterpart
of the assembly line worker, who served as an extension of the machine is the office worker who serves
as an extension of an electronic system. As the
required level of involvement of the computer atten-
dant rigidly fixed in front of a computer screen is
much greater than the assembly line worker, his or
her moment-to-moment awareness of self is corre-
spondingly less. At least on the assembly line, a
worker could daydream or fantasize and exercise
physically.

The market place is no improvement. Marketing managers see the public as consumers of goods;
consequently, they have little interest in people as
unique individuals. In the marketing process, people
are seen as entities who, if properly conditioned by
wish-fulfilling inducements, will purchase products
whether those products are needed or not. Such
conditioning is dehumanizing.

Traditional churches, despite their obsolescence, are still of much value to their remaining
members. These values would be preserved in Contemporary Church. First and foremost, membership
in the Contemporary Church would provide community life. It should be noted that the decline of

church involvement has been accompanied by a great
increase in personal alienation. Extreme manifestations of this alienation in America are the many socially detached people, urban gangs and rural militia
groups. This alienation has been a gold mine for
psychiatrists and peddlers of social panaceas.

Churches have always acknowledged the
common passages of life: youth and old age, birth
and death. The Contemporary Church would also
celebrate these passages but in a way that would
encourage the individual to recognize the uniqueness
of his or her experience. The Contemporary church
would also celebrate political and intellectual developments that have advanced Western civilization.
Along with the Magna Charta, the Declaration of
Independence, and the American Constitution, the
import of the universal laws of nature, the evolutionary foundation of human life, and the genetic and
experiential endowment of the individual would be
continually reemphasized by public acknowledgement.
Church edifices and ceremonies would continue to
incorporate the best artistic expression of contemporary American culture as did the medieval cathedrals
of Europe which were perhaps the finest expressions
of public consciousness by any civilization.

Contemporary Church would be wherein individuals would have the opportunity to experience their human uniqueness. It would also foster awareness of the responsibility to express uniqueness only in ways that respect the uniqueness and rights of others. It would be the shared responsibility of all its members to insure that this mutuality is realized.

The recognition of the infinite variety of human kind should create a very rich and inclusive society. One could honestly declare his or her personality without fear of ostracism if accompanied by acknowledged responsibility for its expression. Dominant types would be encouraged to seek leadership. Acquisitive people would be encouraged to create wealth. The more docile could seek less demanding lives yet urged to retain their responsibility for protecting their own rights by overseeing the more aggressive and acquisitive. Sexuality -not only as male or female- but in its variations of forms and intensities would be acknowledged and assessed in light of the best information available. Even antisocial urges could be revealed when accompanied by commitment to deal with them therapeutically.

Contemporary Church would be predicated on the evolving body of reliable public knowledge; yet it would not make knowledge into dogma. Experiential truth would not need be abandoned by the individual in deference to conventional wisdom, but responsible public as well as personal behavior would need be informed by relevant, reliable, public knowledge. Nor would simple choice of personal behavior based on total accumulated personal knowledge, both conscious and sub conscious -so called intuition- be subjugated to logic or pressure by either group or peer.

Contemporary Church would be organized so as to minimize opportunities for exercise of greed and lust for power. Throughout the course of history, some church leaders have succumbed to greed and lust for power. The medieval popes saw themselves as emperors, and the protestant church leaders worked hand and glove with their respective political regimes -good or bad. Contemporary Church would minimize pitfalls by precluding concentration of monetary and/or administrative control.

A network type organization of the kind used by activist groups rather than a hierarchical one might be appropriate. The role of administrators would be to facilitate rather than to dictate. Electronic communication might be used for inter-community communication and accessing of reliable information -particularly by means of first hand accounts. In the Contemporary Church the ideal would

be equal access to reality for all. The beauty of on-
line communication is that it is possible to avoid
intermediaries that might filter and slant information.
     Contemporary Church would not be politically
or ethically activist, but would energize individuals by
raising their awareness of relationships to self, fellow
humans, and the world at large. Energized individuals
would then pursue their agendas in appropriate are-
nas. Partisan activities within a community are de-
structively divisive; however, inputs from activist
groups could provide information on issues relevant
to the members of the community.

     Groups with particular interests within the
assemblies would work to establish a common ground
endorsed by consensus of their members. For instance, a group interested in the environment -the
self-to-world or universe relationship- would need to
digest a great deal of information and opinion on the
subject to develop a conditional consensus among
themselves. Consensus would be considered to be
conditional as it would always be subject to change
by new information or by changing societal conditions. Group viability would demand a great deal of
patience and forbearance by all participants.

     Group-consensus positions on critical issues
would be from time-to-time presented to the larger

assembly by the focus groups. It would be expected
that the individuals would join a particular group when
their interests in the given subject were somehow
sparked. Similarly, it would be expected that individuals could move on to other groups or to just participation in the general assembly as their interests
evolved.

Traditional churches have never emphasized
one's capacity to resolve one's own problems nor the
power of the society to resolve the problems of
society at large, but has emphasized one's dependence on divine intervention; although, -ironically-
religious leaders have never ignored practical methods in pursuing personal or institutional objectives.
Contemporary Church would encourage the confront-
ing of both personal and social problems as challenges that are best dealt with awareness heightened
by close examination, thorough analysis, and forth-
right action which recognizes the legitimate claims of
all those involved.

The awareness fostered today by the entertainment industry and the advertising establishment
is primarily physical and emotional. Organismic
awareness -that is awareness of one's self as a physical, reflexive, emotional, and cerebral organic entity-
is largely neglected. Traditional church emphasizes a

so-called spiritual awareness of people and neglects their material awareness. Contemporary Church would recognize the broad spectrum of human response to life's situations and the total evolvement of the human organism in them.

Obsolescence is a problem common to all institutions. Dogmatism prohibits traditional churches from accommodating the evolving awareness of its members. Christianity has had arrested development for many centuries. Leaders of all orthodox institutions - institutions claiming infallibility- are eventually plagued by the dilemma of either admitting error or becoming irrelevant through obsolescence of their tenets. Contemporary Church, in contrast, would recognize its own evolving nature.

The pastoral relationship of shepherd and flock would not be the predominant relationship in Contemporary Church. This traditional relationship is tacit acceptance by the flock that they are incapable of being in charge of their own lives. Though this might true to a degree depending on the situation, a person who accepts the role of a member of a flock should realize that he has relinquished direction of his life to another whose legitimate interests are not primarily his own. The model relationship among community members would be one of demonstrable mutual

benefit that recognizes the unique talents of both
and respects the prerogatives of both. Responsibility
and authority would be more diffused in congregations than has been the case. Members of a congregation would see themselves as a self governing
group and would organize recognizing the specific
character and needs of its members.

A Contemporary Church congregation through
its activities and programs would be a functioning
society wherein the self relationships are employed
and refined. Self awareness raising would be an
activity of all age groups. I expect that some interest
groups within the congregation would have an economic focus. Personal money concerns in our society
can not reasonably be excluded from the religious
arena. Of course, social interaction among all age
groups would be a natural expression of community.
Environmental and ecological groups would direct
attention to the world and universe.

The prime function of the Contemporary
Church would be support of religious maturation.
This would differ from religious education in that
indoctrination would be replaced by providing the
environment and information for developing mature
self-to-self, self-to-other, and self-to universe relationships. These relationships would be both those

existing among the Church members and those between Church members and the world at large. All
aspects of the individual's relationship to the market
economy and all aspects of interpersonal relationships would be considered appropriate subjects for
attention. Public institutions and their policies would
also be legitimate subjects for examination.

In addition to groups within congregations,
there could be groups of those who wish to refine
their own self relationships independently of the
larger congregations or be activist in nature yet be
members of their respective congregations. The
members of such groups would decide among themselves format, rules, and the focus of their attention.
The value of a given small group would rest on its
commitment to objective reality and mutuality. Freedom of association -and non-association- and free
expression would be paramount.

These groups would have an essential role to
play. Within the independent groups, information
gathering, dialogue, and additional refinements of the
self relationships could be more energetically pursued
than in a larger body. The heightened awareness
resulting from independent group activities could be
infused into the general membership through individual involvement of independent group members in

the activities of the larger bodies.

Dissident religious groups, -particularly of Catholics - that have come into being during the last twenty-five years, have sought the freedom of religious development independent of the Church. Participants in these groups generally see themselves as being in opposition to the hierarchy of the Church rather than providing an enlightening function for members confined by the hierarchy. In turn, the Church hierarchy gives no acknowledgement of the potentially-important contributions that these independent groups could make to the future of the Church.

Affiliation of local congregations practicing Reality Religion to form a Contemporary Church for American society would require agreement on broad principles. There is precedence for this in protestant denominations. An affirmation of the basic tenets of Reality Religion might be the following statement:

I, as a living organism, am an
expression of the universe. The same
basic forces that drive the universe
underlie my organic functioning.
Though I can comprehend the workings
of the universe on a human scale, as
only part of the whole, I can not fully

comprehend the ultimate mystery of the whole.

I will behave, to the degree possible, in accord with the wisdom of the universe as revealed in reliable human knowledge. I will shun ideologies and both self and public deceptions even if doing so leaves me with degrees of uncertainty.

I will express the attributes of organismic life as they uniquely occur in me and respect like expression in others. I will seek to resolve the conflicts inherent in life in ways that maximize organismic human expression.

Contemporary Church members would recognize that profound and original thinking is done almost exclusively as a solitary activity. The individuals who are creatively active would be welcome in their respective communities even though commonality of thinking might be small. Original thinkers often appear out of step with the majority. This is to be expected; but among those with heightened awareness, others who step to another drum beat would not be ostracized.

Facilitators and directors would be needed at

the congregation level and at the level of the um-
brella organization. Facilitators are the people who
handle logistics and interface with the civil community. Directors are those who organize and execute
programs. All activities would be subject to the
oversight of the general membership. The highly
autonomous nature of local congregations should
minimize the need for hierarchical structure. Opportunities for concentration of executive power would
be minimized by community charters. Ideals of
democratic and transparent administration would be
explicit in the charters at all levels.

Members would accept change as an important
feature in religious life. A balance between rate of
evolving and continuity would be sought that would
allow change yet provide both personal and social
stability. The inertia of the body of public knowledge
would work to this end. Time is required for new
information to be incorporated into public knowledge
and subsequently into public consciousness.

Contemporary Church membership would be
appealing to Americans. Reality Religion can recast
the disturbing personal behavior in our society as the
result of normal functioning of humans without a
religion that provides a rational basis for relationships. Reality Religion would supply the understand-

ing and the responses that would manage these tensions and yet observe the limits of democratic means. Technology which has been seen as a dehumanizing threat would be seen as an asset when employed in a manner to support realization of human potential. Rampant individualism would be tempered by the accountability required by the many who would be aware of the susceptibility of some to unacceptable extremes of behavior.

It might be hoped and even anticipated that availability of a religion based on objective reality and the primacy of organismic human life as the basis of behavior will be obviously superior to those ideologies and dogmas detrimental to American goals. Unfortunately, the latter are harbored by large numbers of people who though living in America have not assimilated American ideals. Absent the undesirable mores of these groups, their traditions of food, dress and art forms would enrich the cultural fabric of the larger society.

What are the prospects for an orderly transition of the traditional churches to a form and structure that is relevant and appropriate in today's America? There is considerable religious foment in America of widely varying types. Fundamentalism is popular among segments of most sects. It is an

antidote to confusion. There are numerous personality cults promising greatly enhanced capabilities to
their members by esoteric mental disciplines. Several
of these cults have surprisingly large numbers of
adherents. Their futures are tied to the fortunes of
their respective gurus. There is little to expect from
these marginal sects; and, unfortunately, the obstacles to transition by the mainstream sects are
formidable and fundamental.

On the religions of some Catholics as well as
members of other denominations are evolving toward
a reality basis. More than a few of those seated in
church pews on Sundays accept little of the official
dogma of their church concerning a non-material
world nor its mythologically-based moral dictates.
Many parish clergy also avoid mythologically-based
topics such hell-fire, heaven and hell in any real
sense, angels, devils, and the array of spirit forms.
The subjects of birth control and remarriage after
divorce -on which the majority of Catholics have
already made up their minds- are similarly avoided.

On the institutional level there are significant
instances of organizations that resemble what I have
envisioned as Contemporary Church. These are
associations of activist organizations and church
congregations both Catholic and Protestant. The

focus is on such things as housing for the poor, food for the needy, reduction of violence locally as well as internationally, neighborhood and community priorities, and family related legislation.

Those in the activist organizations, congregation members, and the clergy have sufficient common interests to work effectively to realize certain specific goals. The activists gain access to what has always been and still is the most coherent and inclusive groups of people in society. Congregation members enthusiastically embrace activities that allows concrete expression of their religious commitment. Finally, the church hierarchies see these associations as invigorating for there parishes and congregations in a time when interest in traditional religion is waning.

There are obvious tensions in these associations. Grassroots organization conflicts with hierarchical organization. One is horizontal and the other is vertical. Additionally, church groups include people with diverse self interests. Some are better off financially than others; some see particular issues from viewpoints differing from that of the activists. Also, there is the issue of division of authority and influence between the pastor and those participating in the action group. Despite these tensions these activist/church member organizations are vigorous and effective.

The participants are expressing by their actions their individual religious principles. In concrete ways, they are expressing their self-to-self, self -to-others and self-to-world or God relationships. This a nation wide phenomenon. Cross fertilization between the activists, congregation members, and the clergy is inevitable. If these associations endure, I can't help but believe that they will effect a transformation of religion in America. But will church hierarchies accept this transformation and will the secular activists be able to manage this transformation to a new American public religion?

The challenge for both enlightened clergy, lay persons, and activists alike who recognize the need for an American public religion is to replace the mythological base for relationships with Reality Religion and yet preserve existing communities and other positive church features. This might not be possible. Christianity which originated within Jewish society did not subsume orthodox Judaism. Reality Religion might likewise be stymied by the orthodoxy of Christian denominations. A new beginning might be necessary.

Changes in public consciousness are always

slow. Even in this day of instant communication, establishing new social norms takes several generations. Examples of changing norms are those resulting from the environmental movement and the feminist movement. The road to a new religious paradigm will be long one, full of twists and turns.

The hierarchies of the mainstream churches see fundamental reform as a slippery slope which could lead to totally destruction of their holds on their respective positions of status and authority. If Church hierarchy would accept the inevitability of change and/or Church members could find ways of preserving communities while driving obsolete Church teachings into obscurity by disregard, time might possibly allow a transition to a new religious foundation; however, this is a very unlikely scenario despite some indications of such developments at the grass roots level.

A popular proposition among Catholics at odds with their hierarchy is that the people are the Church -in one sense an obvious truth. To date, however, there have been only feeble efforts by lay members to actually exert any influence on their religious institutions. Most fail to realize that, in America, most limitations on their powers to influence their religious institutions are largely self imposed. Most dissidents have never tested their power to change their church by open dissent from within.

A immediate course of action for individuals who are at odds with their church institutional leaders would be to selectively choose their involvements within their respective parishes. Each of these involvements would present ample opportunities for sharing one's views with fellow parishioners while supporting only activities seen as positive and ignoring those seen as negative. This approach would provide a great opportunity to test the power of one's ideas and to appreciate the real obstacles to social transformation.

Individuals doing this would need confidence that, if their message is valid, that over time, it would raise the awareness and change the behavior of their fellow parishioners. An advantage of this approach is that it offers the opportunity to effect change while enjoying and preserving communities. A further advantage is that organization of a group effort would not be necessary to the mission.

If a new beginning must be made, the many members of religious dissident and social-activist groups in our society might lead the way. Those who are interested in establishing a common ground for American culture in the next century and millennium, might agree to form Contemporary Church assemblies or congregations -not on the basis of total acceptance of Reality Religion but on the basis of acknowledgement that valid, public knowledge is the only practical common ground for a diverse and conflicted American society. While valid public knowledge can not be definitively stated at any given moment in time, it is a unifying concept that through continuous refinement will provide an ever expanding arena of agreement for people without regard for differences in age, race, gender, or personal political or religious views.

Activists would be asked to leave their special interest agendas at the door, but would be encouraged to participate in consciousness raising within the Church. They could responsibly present to the total membership that reality which is the core of their concerns. Their information would have to meet the criteria of valid public knowledge -that is information verifiable or verified by disinterested parties.

The general meetings of parishes or congregations would focus on the celebration of commonality of perceptions and commitment to establishment of a viable American culture. General meetings of celebration might be monthly affairs; and groups with particular interests -be it youth activities, environment, or education- might schedule meetings at their convenience.

The adolescent population might be introduced into religious community through the leadership of those concerned with the wellbeing of them as individuals and as the future conservators of American society. These activists, teachers, mentors, and advocates would find a hospitable environment in the Church. They could introduce the younger people to a community radically different from what the latter might recollect from their childhood or what their parents knew. It would be one that recognized the challenges of growing up in today's world and that would support responsible and realistic maturing of their self relationships in the community of the Church.

American society will be hard put to survive in an environment rampant with aggressive ideologues and exploiters, both domestic and global, without a viable public religion of its own and an institution to sustain it. Recent history provides many examples of nations that failed because they lost or never had a common religion: Russia, Lebanon, and Yugoslavia -to name a few. Concerned Americans would do well to give high priority to establishing a new public institution which would meet their unique needs for a common culture. This is an appropriate and auspicious time -the turn of the century and the millennium- to begin this work.